Barbara Randle's

CRAZY
QUILTING
with attitude

Published by

krause publications
An F&W Publications Company

700 East State Street • Iola, WI 54990-0001
715-445-2214 • 888-457-2873
www.krause.com

To place an order or obtain a free catalog, please call 800-258-0929.

Editor: Christine Townsend
Designer: Marilyn McGrane

Library of Congress Catalog Number: 2003105296
ISBN: 0-87349-664-7

Dedication

This book is dedicated to my friends, Joan Brown, Celeste David, Becky Jones, and Virginia Lindsay who, from the beginning of this "craziness," have loved this wonderful wacky art as much as I have. And to my many students from all over this country who just keep coming back for more. And to my husband, Ed, who holds my hand, encourages me, and lets me continue this obsession.

Acknowledgments

I am so convinced that my journey has been guided by a higher power. I don't believe it was coincidental that Linda Wright brought Nancy Zieman to my house one day only a short time after I learned about crazy quilting. Nor was it by accident that the American Sewing Guild had their National Convention in Birmingham the next year, enabling me to reconnect with Nancy and meet Linda Lee, Chris Timmons, and Mary Ray. My thanks to all of these wonderful friends for advising, encouraging, and believing in me. Not only did I not believe I could create a book in this lifetime, but never dreamed I would have the opportunity. Thanks to Nancy Zieman for believing that I could do something I wasn't even sure I could do and for introducing Krause Publications to me. Thanks to Julie Stephani at Krause Publications for her patience and for walking me through the process. Thanks to my editor, Christine Townsend, for her assistance and expertise. I am so grateful to my husband Ed Randle for his valuable input; and to my caring and encouraging son, Bill Vandiver, who always shows interest in an art to which I'm sure he really doesn't relate! I would like to thank The Tacony Corporation for the use of the Baby Lock and Elna Machines. I also want to thank Bernina of America, Inc. for believing in me. Last but certainly not least, this book would be nothing without the fabulous photography by Sylvia Martin. It was also no accident that I met her. Who else in the world could practically move in with my family and me a week before Christmas and photograph, process, and deliver the work so that I could meet a deadline of January 1? (Sylvia is another person Linda Wright brought into my life.)

Table of Contents

Projects

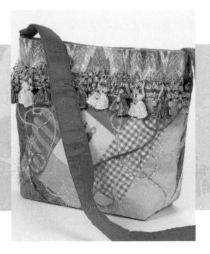

CHAPTER 1

If I Can Crazy Quilt, You Can Too

If you're a crazy quilter, you know that crazy quilting is not new. If you've never crazy quilted, you are probably looking at this book because you are fascinated with the kaleidoscope of color and the creative aspects of the art that you see. In fact, crazy quilting dates back to the late 1800s. Crazy quilts, both antique and current, are incredible displays of creativity, and many times, are reflections of an individual's life. Each piece is unique and reflects the artist's own taste ... no two pieces are completely alike.

In this book, I would like to share with you a fresh, new approach to this wonderful old art. Welcome to the crazy world of the unexpected, stretch-of-the-imagination, color-freedom, whimsy, and "outside-the-box" creativity. It's easy, fun, and stress-free. Anyone can do it. All it takes is desire. You do not have to have experience with a sewing machine. In fact, even if you've never sewn, I promise, if you want to learn, you can. Think of it not as sewing, but as creating your own personal art. If you're an "artist wannabe" as I am, this is just the thing for you.

Sewing has always been a part of my life. My grandmother taught me to sew when I was a child. I don't remember much about what I made, but I do remember the neat little rolls of fabric in her sewing room. They were every imaginable color, print, stripe, floral, dot—you name it. My grandmother sewed dresses for me, and the idea of creating appealed greatly to me.

When I reached high school, I signed up for sewing classes. I paid close attention and learned all I could about stay stitching, basting, using tracing paper and the tracing wheel, pressing seams open, ⅝" seams, blind stitching—all the basics. For years afterward, I sewed clothing until I reached my home-decorating phase. In this phase, I did not sew because I loved it; I sewed because I could, and it made things more affordable. To be frank, sewing home-decorating projects, like dust ruffles, pillow shams, pinched-pleat draperies, slipcovers, and balloon shades, did not excite me. Not surprisingly, twenty years ago, I totally burned out on sewing—this eventually happens when you find yourself doing something you don't love to do. I gave my sewing machine away. I truly felt I would never sew again.

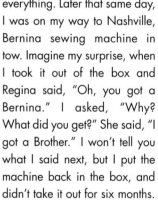

It didn't take long for me to realize I needed a sewing machine again, at least for the odd repair jobs. I purchased a middle-of-the-line Elna 5000. I thought I'd died and gone to heaven, it was so wonderful and easy to use! I began sewing items for my home again. Nothing was too much for me to tackle—I could do anything with my Elna. I even learned how to use the blind hem stitch, making hems look very professional. (Big mistake! Don't ever brag about your hem stitch! Do I need to tell you why?) So, even though sewing was back in my life, I still felt as if something was missing.

I had always dabbled with paint, but eight years ago, I started taking painting lessons. It was my good fortune to find a wonderful art teacher, Linda Vance. Linda is a gifted artist who knows absolutely everything about color. She taught me so much that applies not only to my painting, but also to my sewing. So while painting became my hobby, the sewing embers were still burning: Occasionally I would make window treatments, slip covers or throw pillows. I spent a lot of time helping my friends pick fabric and make decorating items for their homes. Not that I was so good at it, but my services were free and I have always loved working with beautiful fabrics.

A few years ago, I got a call from my Nashville friend Regina Smithson. Regina and I have shared many a sewing project during our friendship. She called to tell me (or so I understood), that she had just bought a fabulous new Bernina sewing machine with all the "bells and whistles." Regina spent the next 20 minutes telling me about everything it would do, and how she had easily learned to use its embroidery module to make monogrammed baby pillows and other wonderful and fun things.

Whenever Regina gets a new or fabulous thing, I must have one just like it (do you have friends like that?). I promptly hung up the phone, got out the phone directory, and found a Bernina dealer. Yes, they did have that particular Bernina machine in stock, they said. So, I bought it that day, and told them I didn't need any training because my friend in Nashville was going to show me everything. Later that same day, I was on my way to Nashville, Bernina sewing machine in tow. Imagine my surprise, when I took it out of the box and Regina said, "Oh, you got a Bernina." I asked, "Why? What did you get?" She said, "I got a Brother." I won't tell you what I said next, but I put the machine back in the box, and didn't take it out for six months.

When I did muster up the courage to take it out of the box, I looked at it and wondered why I thought I needed this machine; what would I ever do with all those decorative stitches? What in the world were all of those buttons for, I wondered … particularly whether the "Smart" button would really make me smart! I honestly was afraid of the machine because it was so expensive. I never did what I was supposed to do—get training from the dealer about how to use the machine. Instead, I would go to the Bernina store and ask a question, get an answer, go home, turn on my machine and go through the motions of sewing. Well, I was doing straight stitching quite well. I learned how to make it zigzag and yes, I figured out the blind-hem stitch. I knew it was a wonderful machine but believed I had bought something too complicated. When I really needed to sew something, I would turn to my Elna because it felt comfortable.

Then, about three and a half years ago, my Atlanta friend Red Buisson called and asked me to help her make throws for a condominium she and her husband were building in Colorado. She asked if I had ever done crazy quilting. Because I had seen old crazy quilts and didn't think they had the look she wanted, my response was for her to come over and let me show her the throws I had been making, combining fabrics in a more "orderly" fashion. (Besides, I didn't know how to crazy quilt.)

When she arrived, she brought with her a crazy quilt throw that her husband had bought for her in Colorado. When I saw it, I knew we were going to learn how to crazy quilt—it was instantly inspiring: A combination of twelve 18" squares, each individually crazy quilted, then attached together, four squares long by three squares wide, and bound around the edges like a "real quilt." Three-quarter-inch gimp was sewn over seams where the squares were joined. The backing was high-quality black cotton. My mind began to click. I could just imagine taking beautiful scraps of tapestries, velvets, silks, damasks, and brocades, then making twelve crazy quilt squares. I would join them like Red's purchased quilt but, instead of bound edges and cotton backing, I would line the throw with silk or velvet and trim the ends with heavy bullion fringe.

Like most people who sew, I have saved fabrics forever. My sewing room is full of fabric leftovers from window treatments, slipcovers, upholstery, and throw pillows, not to mention scraps given to me by my friend, designer Rick Stembridge. I never knew why I was saving all this fabric, but could never bring myself to throw it away. Mostly I just looked at it. Why is it that we sewers just want to have a big stash? Well, at least I knew I had enough fabric to start crazy quilting. The only thing I needed was to learn how to crazy quilt!

Red and I went out looking for a book on crazy quilting. All we could find was a pamphlet-type book with skimpy instructions. To my surprise, the instructions showed attaching the fabric pieces to a foundation fabric. Logic told me that the pieces were cut and sewn together in different directions to achieve the look. How complicated could that be? And, the foundation fabric made sense. The foundation fabric acts as a stabilizer for the individual pieces that turn in every direction. Of course, with such brief instructions, I still had questions.

The next day I returned to the store where I bought my sewing machine. When I asked if anybody there knew how to crazy quilt, a lady who has since become

a dear friend, Virginia Lindsay, said she did. (I later learned that Virginia had won first prize—a serger—for a crazy quilted vest she had sewed, embellished, and entered one year in the fashion show at Bernina University.) With a twinkle in her eye, Virginia sat down at a machine and, using a small piece of muslin and seven pieces of fabric, demonstrated the **sew and flip** technique. After Virginia put about three pieces of fabric together, I had it. I ran out the door, went to a fabric store, bought muslin, and headed home.

My life was forever changed! I am definitely a morning person, and when it gets to be about ten o'clock at night, I'm in bed. But now I was staying up late sewing. I'd try to go to bed, but couldn't get crazy quilting off my mind. One week later I was back at the sewing shop with several 19" squares that I had made using my colorful, textured fabric scraps. Virginia loved what I had done and asked me if (can you believe it?) I would teach her how to do what I had done. I made my first throw within about two weeks.

I was so excited about crazy quilting. It was just what I needed to start really sewing again. And, for the first time in all my years of sewing, I could say I loved sewing. When I sit down at the machine to start a crazy quilt project, I get the same feeling as when I stand in front of an easel with a blank canvas and start a painting. It's so wonderful to combine the fabrics and colors, and to have no boundaries.

Unembellished crazy quilting is interesting and very beautiful because the configuration of fabrics makes each piece different. When I began, I did very little embellishment. But one day I walked into the sewing store and the owner, Robin Parker, wasn't too busy. Of course, she has crazy quilted for years, and she was very supportive of this new journey I was taking. Robin showed how I could adjust the bobbin tension, put heavier decorative threads on bobbins, and use the decorative stitches in my machine to embellish the work from the back. From the day I first learned about bobbin work, my life changed again … I could not believe what I was seeing. I had made this wonderful "cake" of a quilt, and now I had discovered how to put the "icing" on the cake—and it was definitely not plain vanilla icing! Bobbin work was just the beginning; almost a year after I had bought my sewing machine, I found out what a treasure I had.

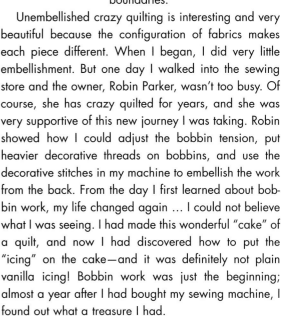

With embellishment, the imagination really goes to work. Machine embellishment is wonderful and quick. The Bernina Artista is the perfect machine for what I do because of the decorative stitches, many of which are nine millimeters wide. It has a removable bobbin case, making the bobbin tension adjustable for use with heavy threads. Hand embroidery is not so quick, but really fun and great to do while traveling. You can embellish with buttons, beads, twisted or braided decorative threads, tassels, prairie points, fabric fans— you name it, the sky's the limit!

As with everything I become enthusiastic about, I *had* to share this with everyone I knew. I called Regina and Red, told them to get to Birmingham. I called many of my Birmingham friends including Becky Jones, Joan Brown, Peggy Chamblee, and Celeste David. I told them: "You've got to see this." Although I showed it to a few people who were not instantly impressed, the Birmingham group, along with Virginia Lindsay and I, began crazy quilting together every Tuesday night. My husband Ed dubbed us the "Sew & Sews." We started out making throw pillows. We have expanded our crazy quilting repertoire to include purses, evening bags, hats, diaper bags, lampshades, jackets, scarves, table runners, place mats, window treatments, and slipcovers.

I had the opportunity to share the crazy quilt **SEW AND FLIP** technique in classes at the American Sewing Guild Sewing Expo in Birmingham, Alabama, in September 2000. With the help of the "Sew & Sews," we sold out all three classes and came away with a waiting list for more classes. It was six months before I could manage to teach another class but, since then, with lots of help, I have taught about ten overflowing classes a month.

Unique about our classes—and something I believe has helped make them successful—is that each one includes a kit with all pre-selected material; all students finish their project. When asked what to bring to class, our answer is "A smile." No one leaves until her purse, lampshade, Christmas stocking, or whatever she's making, is finished. Perhaps equally important is that we allow *no stress*. The class is 100 percent fun. Our attitude is that it's crazy quilting—anything goes; you *can't* mess it up. And we mean it!

The projects in this book are from a few of my classes. Each project includes dimensions or pattern, a supply list and instructions. I hope my designs inspire, challenge, and stimulate you. Treat yourself to a new crazy quilt purse, or make a crazy quilted lampshade trimmed in beads.

Take your time and enjoy the trip. This may well be the most fun you can have with a sewing machine!

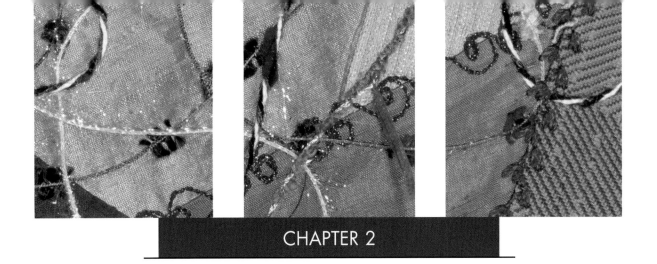

Basic Crazy Quilting

My first thought UPON CLOSE EXAMINATION OF A CRAZY QUILT WAS THAT ONE PIECE OF FABRIC WAS SEWN TO ANOTHER, THEN ANOTHER, AND ON AND ON, UNTIL ALL FABRICS, ALL GOING IN THEIR DIFFERENT DIRECTIONS, WERE LARGE ENOUGH TO MAKE A VERY LARGE QUILT. IT LOOKED A LITTLE OVERWHELMING. AFTER ALL, FABRIC GOING IN ALL DIRECTIONS MEANS THE GRAINS OF ALL THESE FABRICS WOULD ALSO BE GOING IN ALL DIRECTIONS AND WOULD ULTIMATELY STRETCH AND PULL IN ALL DIRECTIONS. WHEN I DISCOVERED THAT IT WAS ALL DONE ON A FOUNDATION FABRIC, IT SEEMED LESS OVERWHELMING. WHEN I DISCOVERED THAT IT WAS NOT JUST ONE BIG PIECE, BUT SQUARES AND OTHER SHAPES SEWN TOGETHER, I KNEW I COULD DO IT. AND YOU CAN, TOO.

Choosing and Cutting the Foundation

The weight of the foundation fabric is dependent upon the project: For lampshades, I use lightweight muslin; for purses, I generally use heavy canvas. For some of my evening bags I use organdy. Stiffer or heavier fabrics provide more body. When you need less stiffness, use lighter fabrics. When in doubt, use lightweight muslin. Add interfacing if you discover, while you are constructing the quilt, that you need more foundation weight.

Always cut your foundation fabric or backing at least 1" larger than your pattern. Some shrinkage usually occurs during the quilting and embellishing processes. After you have finished all quilting and embellishment, and have pressed it all very well, place the pattern on the work and cut. You then have the perfectly sized pieces to make your project. For example: If you want a 13" pillow top (which makes a 12" pillow), cut the muslin 14" square—doing so allows for an inch for shrinkage. Trim the pillow top down to 13" after you have embellished it to provide a ½" seam allowance on each side.

Pressing

One of the most important steps in the crazy quilt process is pressing as you go. To get a smooth finish, I tell my students to make sure the work is as "flat as a pancake" after each piece is flipped and before proceeding with the next strip of fabric. "Little tucks" between fabrics make embellishment difficult and can be unsightly. After finishing crazy quilting, the only way to remove little tucks is to remove pieces. Removing pieces at this late stage definitely slows down the instant gratification process, so do a thorough pressing!

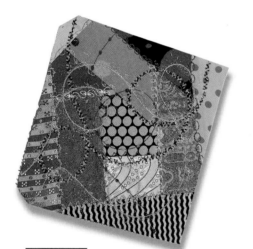

Method 1

Crazy Quilting Instructions

I teach three different methods of crazy quilting in my classes. As you will see, each method is different, although each employs the **sew and flip** technique.

Method 1 is the more traditional crazy quilting method, starting with a central piece then building around that central piece until the foundation fabric is covered. Use this method for pieces that are symmetrical.

Method 2 is the Chevron Design and can start at the center or one corner of the foundation fabric. Use this method for pieces that are asymmetrical.

Method 2

Method 3 is called "On the Slant." Although some may not actually consider this a crazy quilting technique, I have incorporated it into my designs, and use it in many of my advanced classes. It is the simplest of all and goes fast.

Method 3

METHOD 1

The first and most common crazy quilting method begins in the center of the foundation fabric. You can use a four-sided square of fabric, but with a five-sided piece of fabric, the resulting angles create more interest. To make a five-sided piece of fabric, cut a square or rectangle the desired size then simply clip off one corner.

Step 1

Place the five-sided piece onto the approximate center of the foundation fabric and stitch one side only, using a ¼" seam allowance, to the backing. Angle each side of the fabric on the foundation.

Step 2

Cut a rectangle of another fabric and place on top of the first piece where stitched, right sides together. **Sew** the edge just above the original stitching, using a ⅜" seam allowance. **Flip** this piece over to conceal the seam and expose the right side. Press.

Basic Crazy Quilting

Chapter 2

Steps 3 through 7

Apply fabrics using this **sew and flip** method, going either clockwise or counter-clockwise. Be careful to cover all raw edges until backing is totally covered. Trim to seam allowance and press well as you go.

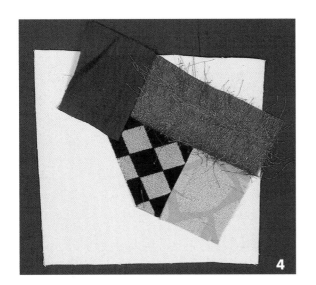

METHOD 2

The second method utilizes the chevron shape; use it for oblong or unusually shaped projects. Start by placing a square in the center of the foundation fabric.

Step 1

Use the **sew and flip** method to go around the square until the width of the backing is covered.

Step 2

Leave each end of this long piece of backing uncovered. Continue the **sew and flip** method until one end of the backing is covered.

Step 3

Repeat for the other end of the backing.

Optional

On certain projects, start quilting on one end instead of the center.

Method 3

The third method is called "On the Slant." I started using this **sew and flip** procedure when I was in a hurry to do a new design. Because you use less fabric, it takes less time to quilt. I use *strips* of fabric only—no centers or squares. Strips can be all one width or cut to different widths to add interest.

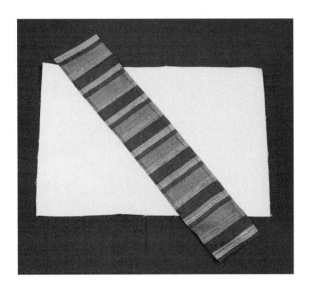

Step 1

Begin placing one strip diagonally from the top left end to the bottom right end of your backing fabric. Stitch both sides of strip to backing ¼" from edges.

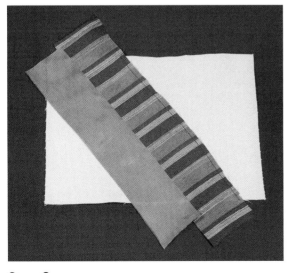

Step 2

Next, place another strip on top of the first strip, right sides together. Sew ⅜" seam allowance from one end to the other. Flip and press.

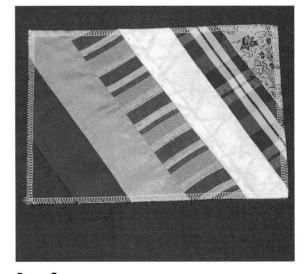

Step 3

Continue to sew, flip, and press until backing is covered.

Adding Interest

Consider pre-piecing strips. The strips may get too long, especially if you are doing large projects. You can sew smaller pieces of fabric together to form the desired length. After piecing these fabrics together, use a rotary cutter and ruler to trim to the desired width and length.

Pre-pieced strip.

Make a row of prairie points

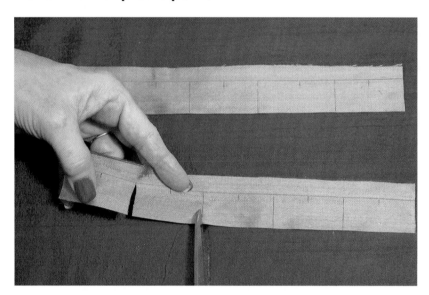

Step 1

For a 10" length of 1" prairie points, cut a rectangle 10" by 3". Fold it in half lengthwise; press on the fold. From left to right edge of fabric, measure and mark every 2". At these points, cut a 1" vertical line.

Step 2

Between the cuts, fold both raw edges inward to form a point. Press. (When sewing these onto your work, be sure to catch raw edges in the seam.) Sew the fold of the points up or down, whichever you desire.

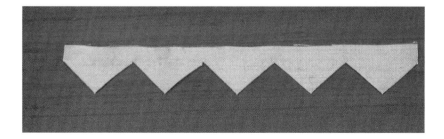

Front of prairie points.

CHAPTER 3

Color Mixing

With crazy quilting, THE RULE *IS* COLOR, AND COLOR IS WHAT ATTRACTS MOST PEOPLE TO IT IN THE FIRST PLACE. HOWEVER, I'VE FOUND THAT MANY PEOPLE ARE FEARFUL OF "BREAKING THE RULES" OR MAKING MISTAKES WITH COLOR. WHEN I TEACH THROW PILLOW CLASSES, I ALWAYS HAVE A FEW NEUTRAL KITS AVAILABLE. THE OTHER KITS ARE JUST OVERFLOWING WITH COLORFUL FABRICS AND TRIM, BUT INVARIABLY, THE NEUTRAL KITS GO FIRST. I KNOW, SOME PEOPLE REALLY DO FAVOR NEUTRAL, BUT MANY OF THOSE WHO PICK THE NEUTRAL TO START WITH COME BACK TO ANOTHER CLASS AND TELL ME "I WANT SOMETHING *COLORFUL* THIS TIME." MY GOAL IS TO HELP YOU GET RID OF THOSE OLD "COLOR INHIBITIONS," AND START HAVING SOME FUN WITH COLOR RIGHT AWAY. YOU CAN ALWAYS GO BACK AND CONJURE UP A REALLY FABULOUS NEUTRAL PIECE LATER (SEE VIRGINIA LINDSAY'S GORGEOUS PILLOW ON PAGE 116 OF "THE SKY'S THE LIMIT GALLERY").

Color is the number one reason I fell in love with crazy quilting—you get to create your own fabric by mixing colors that you love. The colors you choose don't have to match, but they need to balance. For example, if you create a crazy quilt square with red, green, and pink fabrics, but at the very end you add one piece of turquoise fabric, your square might look a little unbalanced in the color department. To balance the color, you'll need to add some kind of embellishment that is opposite the turquoise fabric. You could even leave off the turquoise fabric and have a finished square of red, green, and pink but decide you would like to add turquoise to the finished piece somewhere. Add it with embellishment. Just make sure to balance the turquoise embellishment on your square—in other words, not just in one corner. Remember, this is a piece of fabric that you have created and you can add any color that pleases you. Think about the fabric that you look at in fabric stores. We never question whether a color in a print fabric should or should not be a part of the print. After all, each color of the print is repeated over and over. This is balance.

While it may sound as if I am saying there are no rules when it comes to color, there are, in fact, many rules. If you want to learn about color, study a color wheel or buy a book about color theory. You'll learn that complementary colors—red/green, blue/orange, and yellow/purple—actually compliment each other.

TOP: Aqua, lime, brown, cream, and black color swatches.

BOTTOM: Orange, deep red, cream, and black.

I love to put together unexpected color combinations and, I confess, bright, strong colors are my favorites. Imagine bright aqua, lime green, brown, cream, and black. Or try putting together orange, deep red, cream, and black; purple, marigold, fuchsia, cream, and black; or periwinkle, green, cream, and black. What about putting all pink fabrics together? Most of these color combinations include black and cream. Notice how the black and cream fabric works with the colors. Black and cream work with anything, and actually make the colors happy.

Top: Marigold, purple, fuchsia, cream, and black.

Bottom: Periwinkle, green, cream, and black swatches.

Pink swatches.

I can go on and on about color combinations, but the best way to learn is to experiment. If you want to learn about putting colors together, spend some time in a fabric store. Most fabric stores will give you swatches of fabric—find the colors you love then search for another color that looks great with those colors. Look for textures in the colors you choose. Add a little black and cream.

Neutral swatches.

Another way to create your own color combination is to look through magazines. When you see a picture of a room, floral arrangement, or a garden that you love, pay close attention to the colors in the picture. Find fabrics in all the colors you see.

Remember one thing: When you create a piece of art, it's yours, and you can make it any way, any color, and any size you choose. If you love a color combination, then use it … all God's colors go together. He didn't make any ugly colors and if you will look at His world, He has not been concerned with whether colors match. And yet, the beauty of His creation is everywhere. We never question whether the colors match. Apply this color theory to your projects: "All colors go together to create a beautiful world."

TOP, AND PAGE 18: Floral arrangement from *Southern Lady* magazine (photo courtesy of *Southern Lady* magazine).

BOTTOM: Swatches of fabric to match the floral arrangement from *Southern Lady* magazine.

CHAPTER 4

Selecting Fabric

Shimmery, glittery, glitzy,

FUZZY, FIZZY, SHINY, EYE-CATCHING FABRIC: THE MORE COLORFUL IT IS, THE BETTER. NOTHING GETS THE CREATIVE JUICES FLOWING FASTER THAN A WONDERFUL PIECE OF FABRIC. IT'S LIKE A BREATH OF FRESH AIR, A DRINK OF ICE WATER ON A HOT DAY.

One of my favorite things to do is look at fabric—can you tell? I don't know if it's the wonderful color combinations or the possibilities represented by each piece; all I know is that I love fabric. This is an affliction I had before discovering crazy quilting. When I originally discovered crazy quilting, I felt that a mixture of solids, prints, stripes, dots, and plaids in fabrics such as velvets, brocades, silks, satins, taffetas, metallics, moirés, and tapestries was the way to go. I started out using scraps of these type fabrics and soon found that some fabrics are not suitable. Specifically, heavy fabrics just don't work well for me, so I got rid of all my heaviest upholstery fabric. Tapestries are great if they are not too thick. I love velvet, but it's not the easiest fabric to sew. Designer fabrics made up of cotton and polyester work well. Silks, taffetas, satins, and brocades are always great. There are many novelty fabrics on the market, including some that already have been embellished in some way. I don't use traditional cotton quilting fabric except for lining some purses. On rare occasion, I use pieces of chintz or linen.

I choose fabric mostly by the way it looks, not by the fiber content. If it has the luxurious look I want and isn't too thick, I use it. My goal is to make my crazy quilt projects "sing"; their song is always on my mind as I shop for fabric.

One fabric I'm always on the lookout for is anything black and cream (notice I didn't say black and *white*). For some reason, it's very hard to find black and cream fabric, but as you'll notice, I use it in almost everything I do. When I do find it, whether it is black and cream stripes, polka dots, harlequin, or print, I buy *all* of it. I can't have too much of this magical, neutral combination.

As you travel, use the yellow pages to find fabric stores. There are so many fabric stores and, like everything else, some are better than others; even so, I can always find something I need in any fabric store. Many fabric stores seem to be catering to the fiber artist more than ever before. This is such great news for crazy quilters, because we can now easily find those novelty fabrics, beads, beaded trim, tassels, tassel trim, eyelash trim, decorative threads, yarns, feathers, and much, much more.

If you want to see more fabric and trims than you ever imagined, take a road trip to the garment district in New York. Once there, stroll down West 39th Street—and be prepared to be overwhelmed. Miraculously, some of these merchants will deal with you.

Another great source for fabric is used or vintage clothing. Check your closet for velvet, silk, brocade, taffeta, and any other beautiful fabric from garments that might never be worn again but just keep hanging around cluttering your closet.

Embellishment Material

Embellishment materials are as important as your fabric choices. Many craft shops, fabric stores, and discount stores carry interesting embellishment materials. If you haven't looked lately, check these stores—you may be surprised.

Here's what I look for: Yarns, decorative threads, metallic anything, buttons, beads, tassels, tassel fringe, ostrich trim, beaded fringe, and anything else that I could sew onto fabric.

For yarns, the knit shops are obviously a great place to look. However, many fabric, craft, and discount stores carry yarns. As with fabric, some yarns are more suitable for embellishment than others. For example, heavy, very bumpy yarns don't work as well as thinner yarns for machine application.

A very important yarn is black and white twisted yarn. If that can't be found, any combination of black and white, or black and cream, or black and gray works. Aura, by Trendsetter, would be my first choice for a yarn that works well. It comes in many different colors but gives a wonderful dimension to crazy quilted projects when couched on with monofilament thread. Another great yarn is Flora by Trendsetter or Vendome by Maxime. These yarns have what looks like little butterfly wings spaced intermittently along the yarn. Chenille yarn works very well provided it's not too thick.

For decorative threads, look at fabric or sewing machine stores. My favorite decorative threads for bobbin work are Madiera and YLI. I use these threads in the bobbin for decorative stitches as embellishment on crazy quilted projects.

You can find beads in fabric, craft, and bead shops. Keep in mind the project you're working on when buying beads for embellishment. Since most beads are sewn directly onto the piece, beads that are heavy or that have large holes are unsuitable. I like to use little seed beads in different colors. Since you'll iron your work several times before it is finished, use glass beads (not plastic).

You can find buttons everywhere! And they don't have to cost a lot. Flea markets are great places to find old buttons. If you're like me, you probably have more buttons in your stash than you'll ever use. Go through and look at them again; they may look different if you search through them with a project in mind. Mother-of-pearl buttons are especially nice on crazy quilts … their shine is interesting yet understated and they are thin and lightweight.

CHAPTER 5

The Icing on the Cake

My feeling about embellishment

IS THAT "MORE IS BETTER," BUT IT'S A PERSONAL THING FOR

EVERYONE. SOME PEOPLE LIKE A LOT OF EMBELLISHMENT;

SOME LIKE A LITTLE, AND SOME JUST DON'T WANT ANY

EMBELLISHMENT ON THEIR WORK AT ALL. IT'S QUITE TRUE

THAT EMBELLISHMENT ALTERS THE WAY YOUR WORK LOOKS

BUT, EMBELLISHED OR NOT, FABULOUS FABRICS THAT HAVE

BEEN CRAZY QUILTED ARE FEASTS FOR THE EYES. DO AS

LITTLE OR AS MUCH EMBELLISHMENT AS YOUR INCLINATION

AND IMAGINATION LEADS YOU TO DO.

When it comes to embellishing crazy quilting, the possibilities are as limitless as our imaginations. And, thankfully, there are many sources of inspiration; I continue to buy every book, pamphlet, and magazine I find about crazy quilting. I love to read a wonderful fiber art magazine called *Quilting Arts*. The photography is great and the articles about crazy quilting always inspire me. I am also a very big fan of Judith Montano, who must be the modern-day guru of crazy quilting. She has written many books about it, and the subject of embellishment. Judith's books, and books on crazy quilting by J. Marsha Michler, Janet Haigh, and Alice Kolb, have been my teachers.

While these books and magazines thoroughly educated me about the art of crazy quilting, reading them also sparked the emergence and evolution of my own crazy

quilting style, which is contemporary, and touched with just enough whimsy to tickle the funny bone. I'll confess that my style is also the result of a desire to spend less time hand embellishing—without sacrificing drop-dead results. In other words, I wanted to learn to do the majority of my embellishment *by machine*. Like the art of crazy quilting, these embellishment techniques are not new. I'll share old techniques with you to illustrate how I achieve the look by machine.

One of my favorite embellishment techniques is Reverse Bobbin Work; I don't feel there is nearly enough in print about it (see page 31). Reverse Bobbin Work reveals the true character and boldness of a stitch. Many of the decorative stitches on my sewing machine are modern replicas of the hand-quilting stitches seen on antique crazy quilts. These machine stitches look particularly impressive when sewn from the wrong side of the crazy quilt with heavy, decorative threads, such as Madiera Décor, Madiera Glamour, YLI Pearl Crown, and YLI Candlelight, in the bobbin. Of course, you can sew the same stitches on the front of the work using regular machine embroidery thread in the top and a regular bobbin, but with considerably less impressive results.

Crazy quilted piece without embellishment.

Embellishing Crazy Quilted Work

After I have finished crazy quilting, I steam and press the work to make it as "flat as a pancake." Next, I serge or finish the edges. This holds the fabrics down as I embellish and prevents pieces from being folded the wrong way when I'm sewing from the back. Then I do bobbin work on every seam. After pulling the loose threads from the bobbin work through to the back of the work and knotting them, I begin "driving" (see on page 32). I drive three or four yarns on each crazy quilted piece.

BOBBIN WORK

I do most of my embellishment by machine. As I said earlier, I didn't realize what a wonderful sewing machine I had until I discovered what it could do with heavy, decorative threads in the bobbin. (It is best to have an extra bobbin case that you use only for bobbin work. This way, you can loosen the tension and mark the bobbin case so that it's always ready. Do not adjust the tension on the bobbin used for regular sewing; you could strip the threads on the screw.) I just wind the colors I want onto bobbins, put monofilament thread or matching all-purpose sewing thread through the top of the machine, and away I go.

The first time I tried bobbin work, I couldn't believe the results. After crazy quilting, I turned the work over and looked at the back, and there it was: A roadmap. Each seam is my guide where to sew. Remember, I'm sewing on the back of the work. It's fun to use a different decorative stitch on each seam. Turn the work over to expose the front of the work. The result is a bold stitch, which actually is the bobbin stitch. When doing bobbin work, never back tack. After you have completed sewing the decorative stitch on each seam, pull the ends of the thread through to the back of the work and tie them off to keep them from pulling back through to the front.

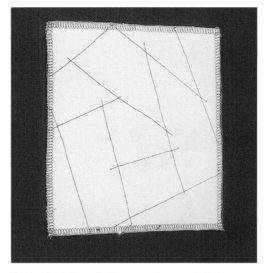

The back of the quilted piece with no embellishment.

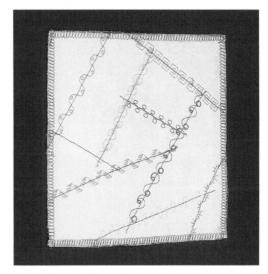

Sewing from the back of the fabric.

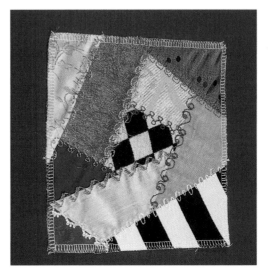

A view from the front.

Driving yarn.

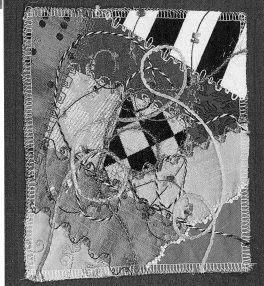

Finished work with four different yarns.

Yarns.

DRIVING

Although bobbin work is dependent upon using good monofilament thread, I still find myself saying: "I hate monofilament thread!" I hate it for the same reason I love it—I can't see it. But if I didn't use monofilament thread, I could never achieve the look of wonderful, colorful threads, yarns, and fibers gliding over my work. Some monofilament threads are better than others. The YLI clear thread works best for me.

Local knit shops are a great source for yarns. Heavy, thick yarns are not suitable, and yarns with large "bumps" are difficult to sew onto fabric. I use Aura by Trendsetter on almost everything—it's glistening with tiny fibers.

For "driving," I use regular bobbin thread in my regular sewing bobbin case, and monofilament thread on the top. My sewing machine is set on zigzag stitch. The stitch width depends on the yarn being couched onto the work. Lengthening the stitch seems to make the process smoother and quicker.

Using a piece of yarn, and beginning at an edge, I zigzag the yarn to the work. (See photo 1.) There is no plan; I just create circles, curlicues, and accept whatever happens. I understand this process is called "couching." When I do it, I feel like I'm driving and totally in control. So, in my classes, we call this method "driving." (For purposes of clarity, "couching" is what I do in the afternoon when I leave my studio and spend time with my dogs; we like to nap on the couch together. Driving and couching are two of my favorite activities!)

BRAID WITH TASSEL

Robin Parker, my local Bernina dealer, taught me much of what I discuss in this chapter. One day when I went into her shop, Robin had a little extra time. She offered to show me something fun. I call this method of embellishment "braid with tassel."

Do this technique away from the edges of your work to avoid catching the braid in the seam allowance. Our example uses a 6" braid, but you can use any length. Use six or eight 18"-long pieces of yarn or decorative thread. Hold them all together and fold at the center. Once halved, they are then 9" long with a fold at one end. (See photo 2.) Using a straight stitch, sew the yarns to your work at the fold. (See photo 3.) You should have 9" of yarn on one side of the presser foot, and 9" of yarn on the other side of the presser foot. Continue to straight stitch onto your quilted piece for about five stitches. Here's where a third hand attachment for your machine is very helpful: Lift the presser foot and crisscross the yarns under the presser foot so that the yarns are now on opposite sides from where they started. (See photo 4.) Lower the presser foot, stitch for about five stitches, and repeat until you've braided for 6". Trim the loose ends to create a tassel. You can add more pieces of yarn and thread at the end to make the tassel more full.

Fuzzy Yarns as Embellishment

Use fuzzy yarns to embellish along a line of your crazy quilting. (See photo 5.) I do not recommend driving with these long, fuzzy yarns, but they look great when used in moderation. Zigzag with monofilament thread, being careful not to catch the "fuzzy stuff" under your stitch. Fluff the fuzz after sewing.

Photo 3

Sewing yarns to quilted piece.

Photo 4

Braiding yarns.

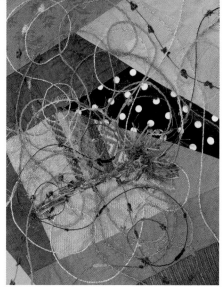

Finished braid and tassel.

Photo 5

Fuzzy yarn zigzagged onto quilted piece.

Flower garden on throw.

Hand embroidery on throw.

Spider web on throw.

BUTTONS

Group some of your favorite buttons together. You can create your own flower garden on your work with buttons and hand embroidered grass and stems. Use different colored and shaped buttons to add interest. Sew them on with different colored thread. When you are sewing them on, string seed beads on your thread to fill the holes in the button.

HAND EMBROIDERY

Hand embroidery looks great on crazy quilting and goes more quickly than you might expect. All of the original old crazy quilts are completely hand embroidered. Many books on the market illustrate hand embroidery stitches. I had not done any hand embroidery for years, but was going on a trip and decided to try. I packed a lot of embroidery threads, needles, scissors, my quilted pieces, and a "how-to" book. I love doing the hand embroidery, because I can use different colors together, and introduce little beads and other treasures onto the quilt. Admittedly, my hand stitching is not perfect, but I get the look I want. Try embroidering a spider web with its own beaded spider, a tree, or ribbon embroidery.

Embellishment is anything your imagination allows. Get creative—try something you've never done before. And when you think you've embellished all you need to on your work, add two more things!

Tree on throw.

Ribbon embroidery on throw.

BEADS OR CHARMS AS EMBELLISHMENT

Hand stitch beads or charms onto your work. Old pieces of jewelry are great sources for interesting beads and other little treasures. Stitch small beads around the print of a fabric or in the center of a flower. (See photo at right.)

APPLIQUÉ

Embellish with appliqué. A fun appliqué is a "Little Person." Look for buttons with faces. If you can't find them, make them yourself: Paint wooden buttons with two dots for the eyes and a half circle for the mouth. Scraps of yarn or ribbon make wonderful hair. Stitch the arms and legs with yarn.

Make a template by drawing or tracing the dress on a piece of paper. Apply fusible web to the back of the fabric. Using the template, cut a dress from the fabric, and lay the dress in the desired position on your work. Place pieces of yarn for arms and legs. (See photo, below.) Fuse the yarn pieces onto the quilted piece. Machine appliqué around the dress. Next, stitch "hair" above the dress, and sew a button on top of stitches where "hair" is attached.

Beads as embellishment.

A Little Person appliqué.

CHAPTER 6

Twenty-inch Throw Pillow

INSTRUCTIONS

1 Using the 4" square and the 3" x 10" strips of fabric, crazy quilt onto the 13" square of muslin. Refer to Chapter 2 for Crazy Quilting Instructions (pages 13 and 14); use Method 1.

2 Embellish as desired (optional).

3 Press well from both sides of work using a pressing cloth as needed.

4 Cut the square down to 12".

5 Hem one side of both pillow backs: Press a ½" hem across one 21" side. Then fold under another inch. Stitch hems. Leave the other three edges raw.

6 Place the crazy quilt square in center of pillow front as shown above. Measure all around to make sure it is centered perfectly. Pin and stitch close to the edge of the crazy quilt square.

7 Starting at the bottom center of pillow front (21" x 21" square), pin cording around edges. Sew cording to square (½" seam allowance).

8 Carefully pin tassel fringe around edges of crazy quilted square, which has been sewn to the pillow top. (The tassel fringe should cover raw edges of the quilted square.) Stitch tassel fringe onto pillow top.

9 Pin the two pillow backs to the pillow front, right sides together, with hemmed edges of these two pieces toward the center. These two pieces will overlap. Note, the first piece that you pin is the piece that will show the most after it is turned right side out; the hemmed edge should be toward the lower edge of pillow. The other pillow back piece is then pinned, raw edge to raw edge, hemmed edge toward the top edge of pillow, right sides together, to the pillow front.

10 Sew, close to the cord, the front to back along pinned edge.

11 Turn pillow cover right side out.

12 Insert 20" pillow form.

supplies needed

- 21" x 21" cut of designer fabric for pillow front
- 21" x 16" cuts of designer fabric for pillow back, 2
- Tassel fringe, 1½ yds
- Cording, 2½ yds
- 13" x 13" square of muslin for foundation
- Fabrics for quilting:
  - 4" square for center
  - 3" x 10" strips of various coordinated fabric, 14
  - 20" pillow form

In my first class, I TAUGHT THE CRAZY QUILT TECHNIQUE. WE WOULD GIVE EACH STUDENT A 13" PIECE OF MUSLIN, A 4" SQUARE OF MATERIAL, AND 14 STRIPS OF FABRIC MEASURING 3" X 10". WE ACTUALLY SPENT THREE HOURS PUTTING THOSE 15 PIECES OF FABRIC ON THE MUSLIN. IF STUDENTS WANTED TO USE THEIR CRAZY QUILTED SQUARE TO MAKE A PILLOW, WE INVITED THEM TO COME BACK TO ANOTHER CLASS TO MAKE A THROW PILLOW. WE WOULD GIVE THEM PIECES FOR THE PILLOW BACKING, SOME TASSEL TRIM AND A PILLOW FORM, AND THEY WOULD LEAVE THE CLASS WITH A FINISHED THROW PILLOW. SOMEWHERE ALONG THE WAY, WE DISCOVERED THAT WE COULD TAKE THE SAME SQUARE AND MAKE IT INTO A 20" PILLOW THAT WAS MUCH MORE ELEGANT. WE NOW DO THIS THROW PILLOW IN CLASS.

THROW PILLOWS ARE GREAT APPOINTMENTS FOR ANY ROOM. HOW WONDERFUL IT IS TO USE LEFTOVER SCRAPS FROM DECORATING THE ROOM TO CREATE THESE ARTFUL ACCESSORIES THAT CAN "PULL IT ALL TOGETHER."

I'VE SPENT YEARS TRYING TO MASTER MITERING CORNERS. SUCH A NEAT LOOK! THIS PROJECT SHOWS A SIMPLE WAY TO GET THE LOOK WITHOUT THE HASSLE OF MITERING.

CHAPTER 7

Neckroll Pillow

Crazy Quilting *with attitude*

- 3" x 21" cuts of designer fabric, 2
- 6½" x 21" cuts of coordinating designer fabric, 2
- Tassel fringe, 42"
- Small tieback tassels, 2
- 9" x 22" piece of muslin for quilting
- 14" x 5" neckroll pillow form
- Fabrics for quilting:
  - 4" square of fabric for center
  - 3" x 10" strips of various coordinated fabrics, 14

Another fun and easy

CRAZY QUILTED PROJECT IS THE NECKROLL

PILLOW. A PAIR OF THESE WOULD BE GREAT AT

EACH END OF A SOFA.

INSTRUCTIONS

Photo 1

Photo 2

Photo 3

1 Beginning with the 4" square and using the 3" x 10" strips of fabric, crazy quilt onto the 9" x 22" piece of muslin. Refer to Chapter 2 for Crazy Quilting Instructions (page 15). Use Method 2.

2 Embellish as desired (optional).

3 Press well from both sides of work, using a pressing cloth as needed.

4 Cut quilted piece down to 8" x 21".

5 With right sides together, stitch 3" x 21" strips to each side of quilted piece. Press seams open. This is the center piece of your pillow cover.

6 Make large buttonholes near the end of both 6½" x 21" pieces. These buttonholes should be perpendicular to each end; place 1" from the end and 2" from the long edge.

7 Press under ½" hem at the 21" edge (this hem is on the edge near the buttonhole of 6½" x 21" piece. Then press under a 1" hem. (See photo 1.)

8 Push tassels through buttonholes from wrong side to right side. Pull cord toward fold. Hem using straight stitch, 1" from the fold with the cord inside hem. (See photo 2.)

9 With right sides together, stitch raw edges of these two pieces to side edges of center piece. Press seams open.

10 Stitch tassel fringe to work even with seam line, joining 3" piece and 6½" piece on each side of the center piece. (See photo 3.)

11 Serge or zigzag raw edges.

12 You now have a piece 20" wide x 21" long.

13 Pin zigzagged or serged edges, right sides together. Stitch ½" seam from one end to the other.

14 Insert pillow form.

15 Draw tassel cords tight at each end.

CHAPTER 8

Little Purse

- Pattern (see pages 123 and 124)
- Canvas foundation fabric:
  - 10¾" wide x 10½" long, 2 pieces for front and back
  - Piece for flap (see pattern, on page 124; cut a little larger than pattern)
- Fabrics for quilting:
  - 4" squares for centers of purse front and back, 2
  - 3" x 10" strips of various coordinated fabrics, 26
  - 2" square for flap
  - 1½" x 4" strips of various coordinated fabrics for flap, 10
  - 26½" x 3½" cut of designer fabric (outer strip that joins front to back; should be medium, not heavyweight, tapestry-type material)
- 25½" x 3½" cut of fusible interfacing for outer strip
- Cording for outer strip, 54"
- For handles:
  - 4" x 36" strips of silk, 2
  - ⅞" x 36" strips of fusible fleece, 4
- Purse lining:
  - Front and back pieces (cut by pattern, page 123)
  - 25½" x 3½" center strip
- Piece for flap (cut by pattern, page 124)
- 13" x 7½" pocket fabric

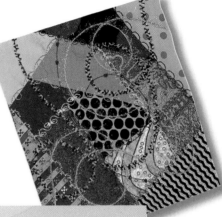

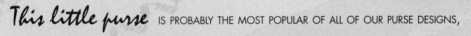

This little purse IS PROBABLY THE MOST POPULAR OF ALL OF OUR PURSE DESIGNS, AND WAS THE FIRST REAL PURSE I MADE. CELESTE DAVID, ONE OF THE "SEW & SEWS," FOUND A PLAIN, LITTLE PURSE WITH SIMILAR MEASUREMENTS AT A LOCAL DISCOUNT STORE FOR $7.00. I MEASURED IT, CUT OUT FOUNDATION FABRIC SIMILAR TO THE MEASUREMENTS, CRAZY QUILTED IT AND ADDED A FLAP, TASSEL, AND BUTTON. WE "SEW & SEWS" CALLED IT "THE LITTLE PURSE." FINISHED, IT MEASURES 8½" WIDE X 9" TALL WITH A 2½" GUSSET.

I MUST SAY IT EVOLVED INTO THE ELEGANT LITTLE PURSE YOU SEE IN THE PHOTOGRAPH. WE THOUGHT THE FIRST ONES WERE ABOUT THE MOST BEAUTIFUL THINGS WE HAD EVER SEEN, BUT WHEN WE LOOK AT THEM NOW, WE CAN'T BELIEVE HOW DIFFERENT THEY ARE FROM THE CURRENT VERSION. THE FLAPS ON THE FIRST ONES WERE A LITTLE TOO NARROW. WE USED TASSELS THAT WERE NOT SUBSTANTIAL ENOUGH, AND IT WOULD NOT BE UNUSUAL TO BE WALKING THROUGH THE MALL AND HAVE THE TASSEL "EXPLODE" AND DROP BEADS ALL OVER THE FLOOR. ADDITIONALLY, WE HAD NOT LEARNED TO DO THE "SUPER PRESS" WHICH IS WHAT GIVES THEM THE CRISP LOOK. I GUESS PRACTICE REALLY DOES MAKE PERFECT ... EVENTUALLY!

INSTRUCTIONS

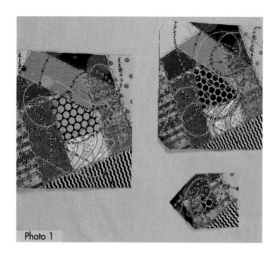

Photo 1

1 Crazy quilt front, back, and flap canvas pieces using squares and strips. Refer to Chapter 2 for Crazy Quilting Instructions (pages 13 and 14). Use Method 1.

2 Embellish as desired (optional).

3 Press well from both sides of work using a pressing cloth as needed.

4 Cut all three pieces down to the size of the patterns. (See photo 1.)

LINING ASSEMBLY:

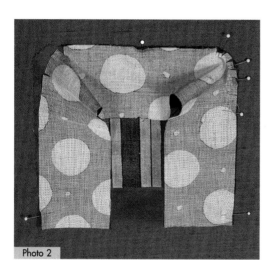

Photo 2

1 Fold pocket in half, right sides together. Stitch around three raw edges, leaving a small space to turn. Turn and press.

2 Sew pocket to the center of lining (back) along sides and bottom of pocket, 2½" from top of lining piece.

3 Join purse lining pieces to the 25½" x 3½" lining center strip. Mark the center of the strip and the centers of both purse lining pieces. Start pinning at the bottom center, matching marks on the center strip to marks on the purse lining pieces. Clip strip to fit around corners. (See photo 2.) Sew the front and back lining panels to the center strip. Very important: Leave an opening across one side of the bottom, approximately 5" wide. This opening is where you will turn the purse.

4 Flap: With right sides together, sew quilted flap to lining, leaving top open. Leave a small opening at point (about ⅛"). Pull tassel cord through opening so that tassel is flush with the point. Stitch tassel cord to seam allowance of flap. Turn and press well. (See photos 3 and 4.)

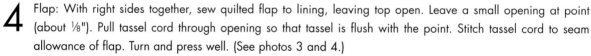

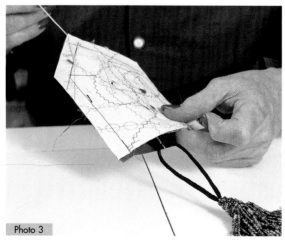

Photo 3

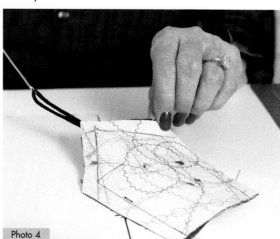

Photo 4

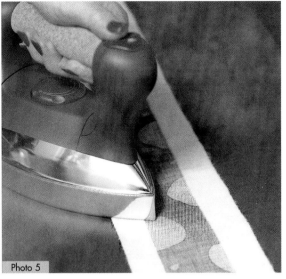
Photo 5

Fusing fleece to the fabric.

Making Handles:

5 Fuse the fleece to each horizontal edge of each 4" x 36" silk strip. (See photo 5.) Fold silk in half horizontally, press. (See photo 6.) Next, fold raw edges with fleece to fold (See photo 7.) Press. Fold in half once more and press. (See photo 8.) Stitch close to both sides from one end to the other. Repeat for other handle. (See photo 9.) Handles measure 1" x 36".

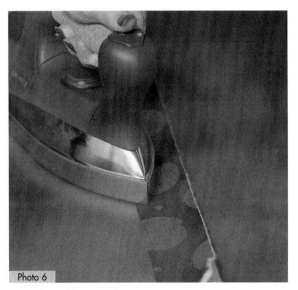
Photo 6

Fabric folded horizontally.

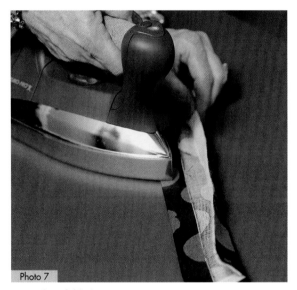
Photo 7

Raw edges folded to center.

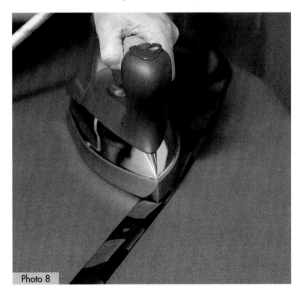
Photo 8

Handle being pressed with both folds.

Photo 9

Stitching handle together.

PURSE ASSEMBLY

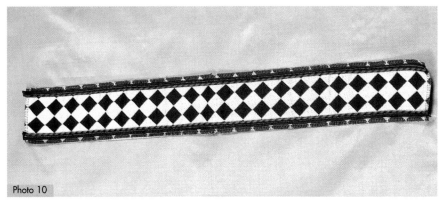

Photo 10

Center strip with cording sewn on.

Photo 11

Center strip clipped to go around corners.

1 To prepare outer strip, fuse interfacing to back of 26½" x 3½" center strip. Pin cording to edges of strip on right side with tape toward edges. Make sure the cording is approximately ½" from edge. This will ensure ½" seam allowance. Sew cording to outer strip using a cording foot. (See photo 10.) Make a mark at the center of the strip.

2 Join quilted pieces to outer center strip. Start pinning at the bottom center as you did for the lining, matching marks on the center strip. Clip strip to fit around corners. (See photo 11.) Sew front and back panels to center strip.

3 Turn so that outer purse is right side out.

PUTTING IT ALL TOGETHER:

1 Pin flap to outer purse, right sides together—center on back panel.

2 Pin raw ends of each handle to outer purse right sides together. Handle ends on back panel should be ⅝" from edge of flap. Handle ends on front panel should match up with position of handle on back panel.

3 Pin lining to outer purse right sides together. Stitch around top of purse using ½" seam allowance.

4 Turn outer purse to outside through opening left in lining.

5 Close opening in lining with top stitching.

6 Steam and press top of purse with lining inside.

7 Top stitch around top of purse.

8 Hand stitch button onto flap above tassel.

9 Press finished purse well.

CHAPTER 9

Modified Myrt
(with Hair)

supplies needed

- Pattern (see page 125)
- Canvas foundation fabric:
  12½" x 11" for front and back, 2
- Fabric for quilting:
  - 4" squares for centers of purse front and back, 2
  - 3" x 10" strips of various coordinated fabrics, 34
  - 29" x 5" cut of designer fabric (outer strip that joins front to back and should be medium, not heavyweight, tapestry-type material)
- 28" x 5" cut of fusible interfacing for outer strip
- Cording for outer strip, 58"
- 36" x 4" silk handles, 2 (see handle instructions for Little Purse in Chapter 8; page 45)
- Purse lining:
  - Front and back pieces (cut by pattern, page 125)
  - 28" x 5" center strip
  - 12" x 7½" pocket fabric
- Plastic canvas grid: 3½" x 9¼" *
- Magnetic snap
- 2" squares of stabilizer for snap, 4
- Crinoline, 4" x 3", 2
- Fusible web, 4" x 3", 2
- "Hairy" trim, 1 yd

  * The plastic grid is used to provide a hard bottom inside the purse. Plastic canvas works well for this purpose. It is available in craft stores.

The Modified Myrt IS SIMILAR TO THE LITTLE PURSE, BUT A LITTLE LARGER. I TEACH HOW TO SEW THIS PURSE IN ALL BEGINNER CLASSES. IT IS A FAVORITE AMONG MY STUDENTS, AND MANY BUY EXTRA KITS TO MAKE MORE OF THIS DESIGN FOR GIFTS. IT HAS A MAGNETIC SNAP CLOSURE. FINISHED, IT MEASURES 11½" WIDE BY 9" TALL WITH A 4" GUSSET.

THE ORIGINAL MODIFIED MYRT DID NOT HAVE "HAIR." THE PHOTOGRAPH AT RIGHT SHOWS HOW "MYRT" LOOKS WITHOUT HAIR.

INSTRUCTIONS

1 Crazy quilt front and back canvas pieces using squares and strips. Refer to Chapter 2 for Crazy Quilting Instructions (pages 13 and 14). Use Method 1.

2 Embellish as desired (optional).

3 Press well from both sides of work using a pressing cloth as needed.

4 Cut front and back pieces down to the size of the pattern.

LINING ASSEMBLY:

1 Fold pocket in half right sides together. Stitch around three raw edges, leaving a small space to turn. Turn and press.

2 Pin pocket onto back of purse lining, centered 2½" below the top edge. Stitch around sides and bottom.

3 Apply magnetic snaps as shown in the photos below. Because of the constant pulling of the snaps, I use interfacing to stabilize the area to which the snap is applied. Center the female side of magnetic snap 1½" below the top edge of lining (above pocket), using two small pieces of interfacing on the inside of lining to secure. Apply the male side of the snap 1½" below top edge of lining (front lining piece), using two small pieces of interfacing on the inside of the lining to secure.

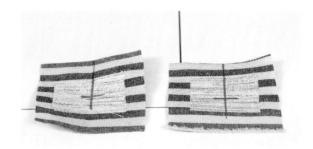

Interfacing fused to material where snap will be applied.

Using the back part of snap as a template to mark where slits should be cut for prongs of snap.

Cutting slits where marks were made with seam ripper.

Finished snap (one side) from the right side.

The four components of a magnetic snap.

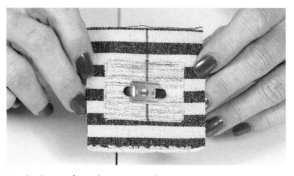

Finished snap from the wrong side.

OUTER PURSE ASSEMBLY:

1 On the inside of crazy quilted pieces, make a mark at bottom centers.

2 To force the center strip to pleat inward at the purse opening, use crinoline as follows: Apply fusible web to one side of each crinoline piece. Fuse crinoline to ends of center strip inside seam allowance. Fold center strip in half, right sides together at ends, and press crease at the center.

3 Fuse 28" x 5" piece of interfacing to the inside of the 29" x 5" outer strip.

4 Pin cording to each long edge of strip on right side with tape toward edges. Make sure the cording is approximately ½" from edge. This will ensure ½" seam allowance. Sew cording to outer strip using a cording foot. Make a mark across the center of the strip.

5 Join quilted pieces to outer center strip. Start pinning at the bottom center, matching marks on the center strip. Clip strip to fit around corners. Sew front and back panels to center strip.

6 Turn so that outer purse is right side out.

PUTTING IT ALL TOGETHER:

1 With right sides together, pin each handle end to top edge of outer purse 2" from side seams. Machine baste handles to purse.

2 With right sides together, pin top edge of lining to top edge of outer purse. Stitch lining to purse. Turn through opening left in lining.

3 Insert grid through opening. Grid will lie at the bottom of the purse between lining strip and outer strip.

4 Top stitch opening in lining closed.

5 Press and steam top edge of purse.

6 Top stitch close to edge of purse opening using edge foot.

More about "Myrt"

BELOW IS ANOTHER VERSION OF THE MODIFIED MYRT. IT'S SIMILAR TO THE ONE IN THIS CHAPTER, EXCEPT THAT I CUT AND HEMMED TWO SILK PIECES ABOUT 9" WIDE BY 15" LONG, AND SEWED ONE ACROSS THE TOP FRONT OF THE BAG AND ONE ACROSS THE TOP BACK OF THE BAG. THIS GIVES THE APPEARANCE OF A SCARF. TIE THE TWO PIECES TOGETHER ACROSS THE TOP. THIS PURSE WAS SEWN AND MACHINE EMBELLISHED ON THE ELNA 6005 MACHINE. YES, I DID BOBBIN WORK WITHOUT A BOBBIN CASE AND IT WORKED GREAT!

CHAPTER 10

Pick Sac
(with One Handle)

supplies needed

- Pattern (see page 127)
- Muslin for foundation fabric, 9" x 14½", 2
- Fabrics for quilting:
  - 17" x 4" strips, 2
  - 13" x 3" strips, 4
  - 10" x 3" strips, 8
- Purse lining fabric, 28" x 13½"
- Pocket lining fabric, 8½" x 14½"
- Outer pocket lining fabric, 8" x 13½", 2
- Purse body fabric: 12½" x 13½", 2 (If you want the inverted triangles in the center of the top edges, cut the triangle in the center 2½" deep and 2" wide.)
- Interfacing for purse body (optional), 8" x 13½"
- Purse bottom fabric, 5" x 13½"
- Silk for handle, 6" x 36"
- Fusible fleece for handle, 1-3/8" x 36", 2
- Plastic canvas grid: 3¾" x 7½" *
- Novelty trim, 27"
- Beaded trim, 27"
- Beaded tassel or weight
- Woven cord, 12"
- Magnetic snap

* The plastic grid is used to provide a hard bottom inside the
purse. Plastic canvas works well for this purpose. It is
available in craft stores.

I was trying to come up with a name FOR THE FIRST DESIGN OF THIS BAG. IT JUST LOOKED LIKE A POUCH, AND WAS A LITTLE DEEPER THAN THE OTHER BAGS. ONE EVENING, AFTER A LONG DAY OF CLASSES AND CUTTING FABRIC, I WAS HALF-COMATOSE ON THE SOFA AND A WOMAN ON TELEVISION TALKED ABOUT THE "PICK-SACK" THAT SHE USED AS A CHILD TO PICK COTTON. THAT WAS IT! I DECIDED RIGHT THEN THAT I WOULD CALL THIS BAG THE PICK SAC.

WHEN FINISHED, IT MEASURES 12½" WIDE BY 11½" LONG. THE BODY OF THE PURSE IS A SOLID FABRIC. THE TWO OUTER POCKETS, ONE ON THE FRONT AND ONE ON THE BACK, ARE LINED QUILTED PIECES TRIMMED AT THE TOP WITH A NOVELTY FRINGE. IT HAS A SINGLE HANDLE, WHICH EXTENDS FROM ONE SIDE SEAM TO THE OTHER, MEASURING 1½" x 36". THE PURSE SHOWN HAS INVERTED TRIANGLES CUT OUT OF THE TOP EDGES OF THE PURSE. YOU CAN MAKE THIS PURSE WITH THE TRIANGLES CUT OUT OR WITH A STRAIGHT EDGE AT THE TOP.

INSTRUCTIONS

MAKE OUTER POCKETS:

1 Using half of the fabric strips, quilt "On the Slant" (see chapter 2, Method 3, on page 16) onto foundation fabric starting in the center with 17" x 4" strip. **Sew and flip** 13" x 3" pieces on each side of center strip. Continue with remaining strips until the foundation fabric is covered. Trim and press.

2 Embellish as desired (optional). Press well from both sides after embellishment.

3 Trim these two pieces down to 8" x 13½". Pin novelty trim(s) along one 13½" edge of each quilted piece. Machine baste close to raw edge. This is the top of pocket. Apply snap to one pocket only: Center male side of magnetic snap (see page 50) 1¼" below top edge of outer pocket lining (top edge is 13½" wide). Use small piece of interfacing on inside to secure. Pin outer pocket lining right sides together to same edge with novelty trim. Stitch across this edge only using ½" seam allowance. Turn right side out. Press. The pocket is now finished across the top and open on sides and bottom. With wrong sides together, machine baste (or serge) the sides and bottoms of these pieces close to raw edge.

PURSE ASSEMBLY:

1 Match bottom edge of each outer pocket to bottom edge of each purse body piece, lining side of pocket together with right side of purse body. Attach along sides and bottoms using ¼" seam. With right sides together, sew purse bottom fabric to lower edge of purse body. Sew other edge of purse, bottom to lower edge, of other purse body. Press seams open. At this point, you should have one long piece measuring 28" x 13½". (See photo 1.)

2 Fold 28" x 13½" piece in half right sides together, matching top edges. Sew along side edges from top to bottom. At the fold, make a clip to the seam on both sides. (See photo 2.) Press side seams open. Miter each side at fold. To form the miter, hold the seam at the fold with one hand and match the center of the seam to the center of the purse bottom. (See photo 3.) This will form a triangle. Pin to hold this position. Measure 2" from point. Stitch across open seams. (See photo 4.)

3 Turn purse right side out.

4 Apply female side of snap (see page 50) to purse body matching with other side of snap, which was applied to outer pocket. Secure with interfacing on inside if needed.

5 Set aside.

Photo 1

Outer purse before being sewn together.

Photo 2

Clipping the bottom.

Photo 3

Stitching across miter.

Photo 4

Hand inside purse forming miter.

LINING ASSEMBLY:

1 Fold pocket fabric in half, with right sides together. Stitch around three raw edges, leaving a small opening to turn. Turn and press.

2 Stitch pocket to lining: Center pocket 3¼" below top edge of one end of lining piece.

3 Fold lining in half, right sides together, matching top edges. Sew along one side edge from top to bottom. Sew other side edge together as follows: 4" from fold and 2½" from top edge. You are leaving an opening through which to turn the purse. Clip to the seam on both sides as you did for outer purse. Miter each side at fold. Sew across mitered triangles 2" from the point.

4 To make a pocket inside lining across bottom to hold grid (this step is optional): Cut a piece of any light fabric 5½" x 8". With wrong side out, press bottom rectangle from miter on one side of lining to miter on other side of lining. Lay creased edge on top of 5½" x 8" piece of fabric. Fabric should extend about ¾" from creased edge. Stitch along fabric using hem stitch.

MAKE HANDLE:

Make the handle the same as the handles for the Little Purse, Chapter 8 (see page 45), were made. Note that this purse is designed for a single handle instead of double handles. The silk measures 6" and the two pieces of fleece 1⅜", which results in a 1½" handle.

PUTTING IT ALL TOGETHER:

1 Fold woven cord in half. Loop through beaded weight or attach beaded weight to folded end of cord. (See photo 5.)

2 With both ends of cord lying side by side, baste raw edges of cord to the point of the inverted triangle in the center back of purse body. (See photo 6.)

3 Pin each end of the handle to the upper sides of the purse, raw edge to raw edge; center at side seams. Machine baste to outer purse ¼" from edge.

4 Drop outer purse (with cord and weight and handles) into lining; lining and purse right sides together. Stitch around top opening of purse. Reinforce woven cord by stitching inside seam allowance.

5 Clip seam as needed.

6 Turn purse right side out through opening left in lining.

7 Press around top edge.

8 Slide grid into pocket in bottom of lining or, if you didn't make a grid pocket, just place grid in bottom of purse.

9 Top stitch opening in lining closed.

10 Top stitch around the top of the purse.

Photo 5

Beaded weight with cord.

Photo 6

Weight basted to right side of purse, and handle pinned to right side of purse.

CHAPTER 11

Night Bloomer Evening Bag

- Pattern (page 126)
- Organdy for foundation fabric: cut ½" larger than the pattern, 4
- Fabrics for quilting:
  - 3" squares of silk, 4
  - 2½" x 6" strips of fabric, 36 (4 each of 12 different fabrics)
- Purse lining, 4 pieces cut by pattern
- Petal: 4 pieces cut by pattern
- Petal lining: 4 pieces cut by pattern
- Interfacing for petal: 4 pieces of lightweight interfacing (muslin can be used)
- Cord for handle, 54"
- Cord for drawstring, 24"
- Small tassels for ends of drawstrings, 2
- Large tassel for bottom of purse
- Novelty trim, 22" cut into 5½" pieces for petals
- Crystals, 4
- Colorful beads, 4
- Tiny round beads, 4
- 1½" to 2" headpins, 4 (for the beads)

This little treasure

IS A PIECE OF ART TO COMPLEMENT THAT SPECIAL EVENING OUTFIT. THE PURSE SHOWN IS MADE OF ALL SILK FABRICS. IT MEASURES APPROXIMATELY 12" LONG FROM THE TOP OF THE PURSE TO THE BOTTOM OF THE TASSEL (TASSEL IS 6" LONG!) THE PURSE BODY CONSISTS OF FOUR CRAZY QUILTED PANELS. THE FOUR PETALS ARE 6" LONG, EMBELLISHED WITH WONDERFUL CONFETTI TRIM, AND FINISHED WITH CRYSTALS AND BEADS AT THE POINTS. IT HAS A CORD HANDLE AND A DRAWSTRING WITH TINY TASSELS.

Night Bloomer.

INSTRUCTIONS

Precision is most important in constructing this purse; everything must be perfectly aligned, and seam allowances must be accurate. Use a ½" seam allowance unless otherwise specified.

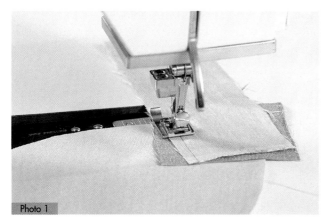

Photo 1

Beginning of quilting.

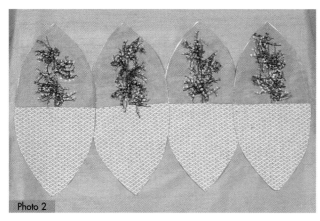

Photo 2

Purse lining pieces sewn to each petal piece.

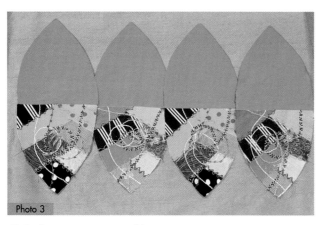

Photo 3

Quilted pieces sewn to petal lining pieces.

1 Crazy quilt four foundation pieces. Use Method 2 (page 15) for quilting. Start quilting with the 3" square positioned diamond shape at the point of the foundation fabric. (See photo 1.)

2 Embellish as desired (optional).

3 Press well.

4 Cut all four finished pieces by pattern.

5 Sew each interfacing to each petal, wrong sides together, using ¼" seam allowance.

6 Stitch novelty trim to center of petal starting at straight edge and ending toward point. (Novelty trim will not extend all the way to the point.)

7 With right sides together, sew each purse lining piece to each petal piece along straight edge. You will end up with four "football" shaped pieces. (See photo 2.)

8 With right sides together, sew each crazy quilted piece to each petal lining piece. You will end up with four "football" shaped pieces. (See photo 3.)

9 To make sure seam allowances are accurate, mark ½" seam allowance from top to point on wrong side of each crazy quilted piece.

10 With right sides together, pin two of the crazy quilted pieces together along marked lines. Carefully stitch along marked line beginning at stitch line at top and ending just before the lines cross at the point. (Ending just before the lines cross will leave a small opening through which you can pull the tassel.) Be sure to back tack seams at beginnings and endings. Petal linings, which were previously attached to each of these crazy quilted pieces, remain loose at this time—do not sew them yet. (See photo 4.)

11 Repeat previous step until all four crazy quilted pieces are sewn together.

12 Pull tassel through small opening where four points meet. (See photo 5.)

13 Secure tassel by stitching tassel cord to seam allowance.

14 With right sides together, pin two of the purse lining pieces along curved edges from seam line at top to point. Stitch from that seam line to point.

15 Repeat previous step until all four purse lining pieces are sewn together. Important: Leave an opening in one of the seams. The purse will be turned through this opening.

16 One at a time, pin each petal lining piece to each petal, right sides together. Stitch each petal, beginning 1" above seam line that joined petals to purse, and ending at point. Be sure to back tack.

Photo 4

Sewing quilted pieces together.

Photo 5

Pulling tassel through opening.

Photo 6

Pinning handle between two petals.

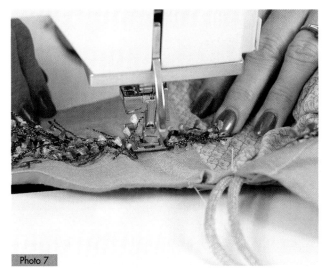

Photo 7

Stitching pocket to hold drawstring.

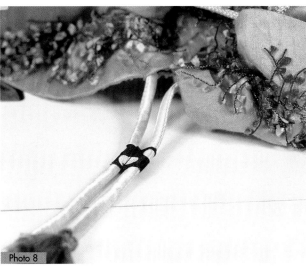

Photo 8

Ribbon slide.

17 Turn purse right side out through the opening left in the lining.

18 Press well.

19 Top stitch opening in lining closed.

20 Pin handle ends down into purse between two petals and opposite between two petals. (See photo 6.)

21 Stitch in the ditch (machine stitch through all layers along the seam lines) all the way around opening of purse.

22 Stitch 1" above ditch on each petal to create a pocket to hold drawstring. (See photo 7.)

23 Pull drawstring through pocket.

24 Hand stitch tassels to ends of drawstring.

25 For a ribbon "slide" which secures the drawstring: Sew one end of a small piece of ribbon around one drawstring and then sew the other end of the ribbon around the other drawstring. This creates a tight "slide" that keeps the drawstring from pulling back through the bag. (See photo 8.)

Crazy Quilting *with attitude*

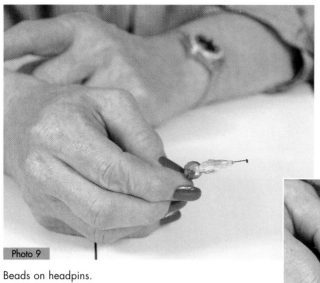

26 Thread beads onto headpins. Loop headpin through point of each petal. (See photo 9.)

Photo 9

Beads on headpins.

Close-up of beads on tips of petal.

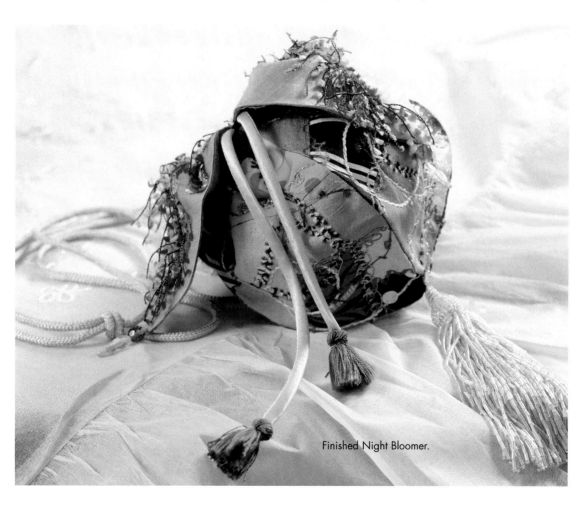

Finished Night Bloomer.

CHAPTER 12

Lampshade

- Muslin foundation fabric
- Square of silky material for center, 4"
- 3" x 10" strips of silky material, 21
- Gimp, or other trim, for top and bottom of shade
- Beaded trim for bottom of lamp
- Sticky lampshade
- Glue gun and hot glue

The lampshade shown IS 4" X 11" X 7". IT IS A SELF-ADHESIVE SHADE AND CAN BE FOUND IN MANY DIFFERENT SIZES IN CRAFT AND FABRIC STORES. THESE SHADES COME WITH A PAPER WRAPPER THAT, WHEN REMOVED, CAN BE USED FOR A PATTERN. THIS IS A QUICK AND EASY WAY TO CUSTOMIZE A LAMPSHADE TO MATCH ANY INTERIOR. TRIMS ARE HOT-GLUED ONTO THE LAMPSHADE.

FABRIC IS A CONSIDERATION WHEN MAKING A LAMPSHADE. THIN FABRICS THROUGH WHICH LIGHT CAN SHINE ARE BEST. MY FAVORITE IS SILK. WHEN IN DOUBT ABOUT A FABRIC, SIMPLY HOLD IT UP TO A WHITE LAMPSHADE WITH THE LIGHT TURNED ON AND YOU'LL INSTANTLY KNOW WHETHER IT WILL WORK OR NOT.

Photo 1

First piece on lampshade muslin.

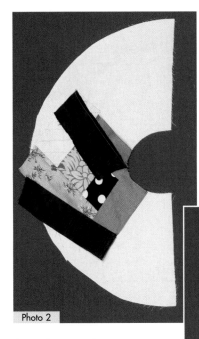

Photo 2

An angle-sewn strip.

INSTRUCTIONS

1 Remove the paper wrapper from the lampshade. (Keep the shade away from excess threads and "fuzz"; once stuck to the shade, they're virtually impossible to remove.) Lay the paper wrapper on the foundation fabric as a cutting guide. Cut muslin at least 1" larger than the wrapper. Put the wrapper back on the lampshade to keep it clean while you work. You will need the wrapper later.

2 Place the 4" fabric square in the center of the muslin on point. (See photo 1.)

3 Use the **sew and flip** method of crazy quilting, going counterclockwise until the square is surrounded by strips of fabric. It gets a little tricky after the first five pieces. Use chevron Method 3 (see page 16) of fabric placement. Press very well as you go. It will be necessary to overlap more than just a seam allowance as you are covering a curved foundation. (See photos 2 and 3.)

4 Important: Trim all excess fabrics and threads as you go. Remember, when the light is turned on, each little piece of thread or bit of fabric will show. Make sure the fabric edges are straight.

5 After covering the foundation fabric, do any decorative embellishment that you desire (optional). Press well again after you have finished embellishing.

Photo 3

Same strip in 12-3, flipped.

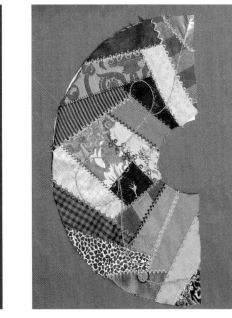

Finished lampshade cover.

6   Take the paper wrapper off the lamp-shade. This is your pattern. Lay it on top of the quilted piece. Cut about 1" longer than the pattern at each end. Cut top and bottom of work by pattern.

7   Press a ½" hem at one end of the crazy quilted piece.

8   Remove all excess threads and lint from both sides of work.

9   Starting at the seam of the shade, finger press the crazy quilted shade cover to the shade, beginning with the end of the crazy quilted piece that is not turned under. (See photo 4.)

10 Smooth as you go. This is why steaming and pressing the work, as you sew and after work is finished, is so important. When the entire piece is adhered to the shade, overlap the raw end with the end that was pressed under. (See photo 5.)

11 With glue gun, glue ends of crazy quilted piece together. Note: The low-temp glue guns work great and save hands from painful burns.

12 Trim crazy quilted piece flush with top and bottom edges of shade.

13 Starting at seam, glue gimp or other trim around the top of the shade. (See photo 6.) Butt the ends of trim together to avoid unnecessary thickness.

Photo 4

Shade as cover is being adhered.

Photo 5

Shade with cover on.

Photo 6

Gluing trim to the top of the shade.

Photo 7

Gluing beads to the shade bottom.

14 Starting at the seam, glue beads around the bottom edge of the shade covering raw edges. To finish, glue gimp or other trim on top of bead ribbon. (See photos 7 and 8.)

Photo 8

Gluing trim above beads on the shade.

Photo courtesy of *Southern Lady* magazine.

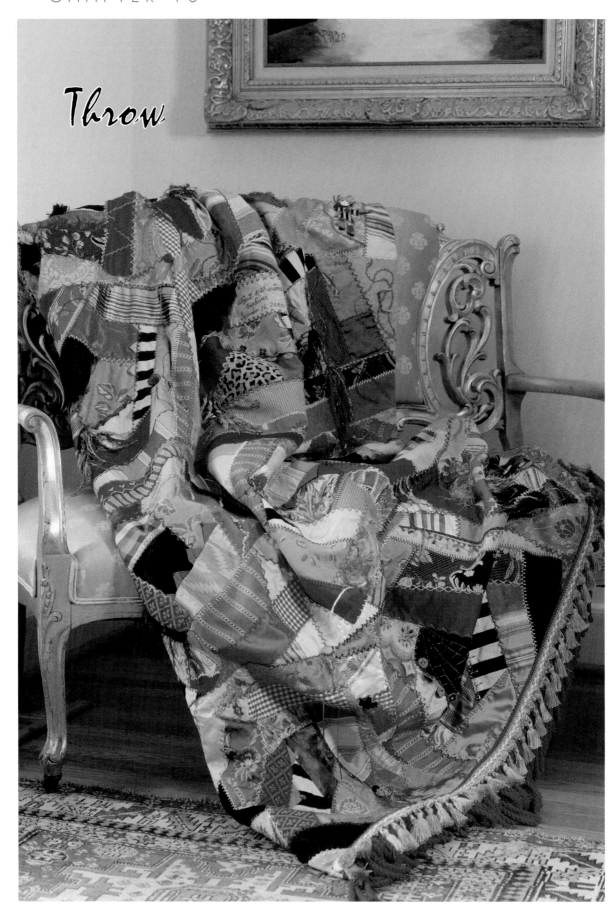

CHAPTER 13

Throw

- 20" squares of muslin, 12
- 5" squares of fabric for quilting, 12
- ⅜ yard of 24 different fabrics cut into 3" strips
- 54" lightweight fabric for backing, 2 yds
- Bullion fringe, 3 yds
- Various embellishment threads and yarns

My crazy quilting journey HAS BEEN A TERRIFIC TRIP. THE BEST PART IS SHARING WITH OLD FRIENDS AND MEETING NEW FRIENDS WHO WANT TO LEARN. THE WORST PART HAS BEEN HOW BUSY IT HAS MADE ME, AND HOW I DON'T SEEM TO HAVE TIME TO ENJOY THESE FRIENDS AS I WOULD LIKE. I WANT TO "SIT AND SEW" TOGETHER AND THEN "DO LUNCH."

IT CAME TO ME RECENTLY THAT IT WOULD BE FUN TO START A SEWING GROUP; MAYBE ONE FRIDAY MORNING A MONTH, I COULD INVITE THOSE WHO WOULD LIKE TO MAKE A 20" SQUARE. WE COULD EACH MAKE A 12-MONTH COMMITMENT TO DO A SQUARE A MONTH, AND AT THE END OF THAT YEAR, WE WOULD PUT THE SQUARES TOGETHER TO MAKE A THROW, JUST LIKE THE ONE I DID WHEN I FIRST STARTED. WE COULD CRAZY QUILT AT MY STUDIO, AND OUR HOMEWORK WOULD CONSIST OF EMBELLISHMENTS ... SURELY WE COULD EMBELLISH ONE SQUARE EACH MONTH.

I HOPED I COULD INTEREST 12 TO 15 PEOPLE, AND CASUALLY MENTIONED THIS TO A FEW PEOPLE IN MY CLASSES. FIFTY PEOPLE PROMPTLY SIGNED UP FOR THE SQUARE-OF-THE-MONTH CLASS. THEY WERE SO EXCITED ABOUT THE IDEA, I REALIZED I WAS GOING TO HAVE TO HAVE *FIVE* CLASSES A MONTH. WE ARE RIGHT IN THE MIDDLE OF THIS "CRAZINESS" AND, AS I WRITE THIS CHAPTER, WE HAVE FINISHED SEVEN MONTHS AND SEVEN SQUARES.

THESE CLASSES ARE SO MUCH FUN AND SUCH A LEARNING EXPERIENCE FOR EVERYONE, ESPECIALLY ME. I WOULD LIKE TO SHARE WITH YOU (SEE PAGES 72 THROUGH 81) SOME OF THE SQUARES THAT HAVE BEEN DONE IN MY CLASSES. THE EMBELLISHMENTS THAT COME IN EACH MONTH ARE BEYOND MY WILDEST EXPECTATIONS. SOME MONTHS, MY FRIENDS WILL DO THE QUILTING AT HOME AND SIT AND HAND-EMBELLISH TOGETHER IN CLASS.

INSTRUCTIONS

1 Using crazy quilting Method 1 from Chapter 2 of this book (see pages 13 and 14), crazy quilt each 20" square. Embellish as desired.

2 Press each square well after all embellishment is finished, and cut to 19" square.

3 With right sides together, sew squares together using ½" seam allowance. The throw will be three squares wide and four squares long. Press all seams open. Embellish these seams as desired.

4 With right sides together, sew lining fabric to quilted throw front. Sew front to back using ½" seam allowance. Add bullion fringe to each end.

Sandra Morgan

Sandra
Morgan

Barbara Durrett

Becky Jones

*Suzzane
Waid*

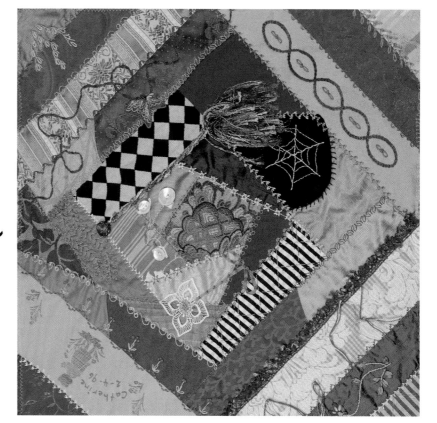

Eleanor Key

Suzzane Waid

Eleanor
Key

Patty
Vann

Eleanor
Key

Linda
Sims

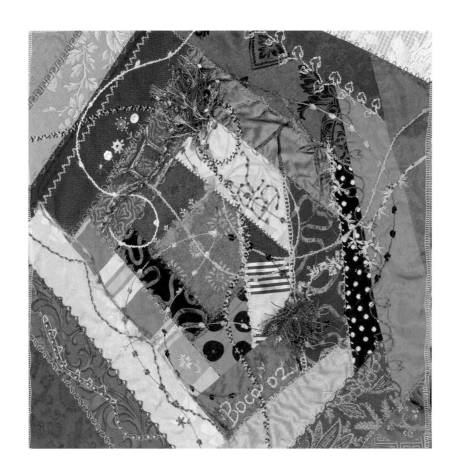

Barbara
Randle

Patty
Vann

Suzzane
Waid

Linda
Sims

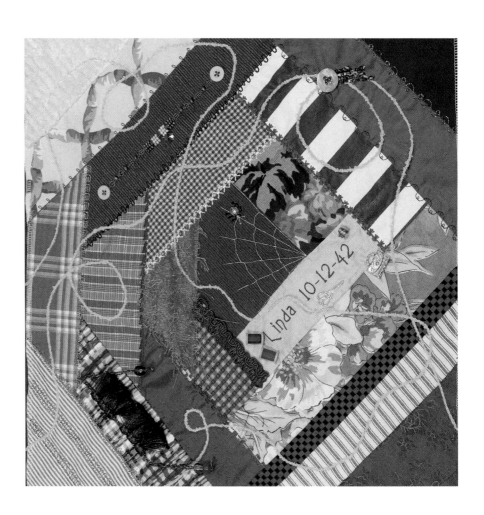

Crazy Quilting *with attitude*

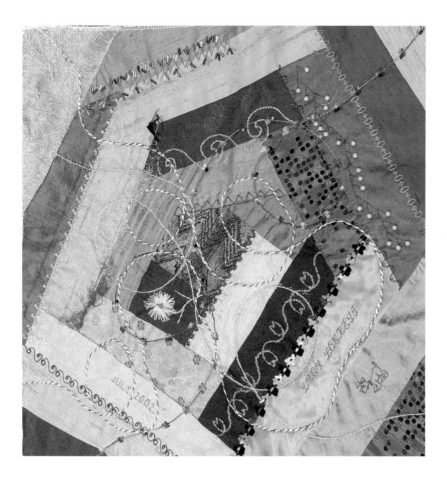

Becky
Jones

Linda
Sims

CHAPTER 14

Six Crazy Quilt Projects

Now that you have the hang OF THE **SEW AND FLIP** PROCEDURE AND OTHER CRAZY QUILT TECHNIQUES, I CHALLENGE YOU TO TRY ONE OR ALL OF THE SIX PROJECTS PRESENTED IN THIS CHAPTER. I'VE INCLUDED THE DIRECTIONS, DIMENSIONS, OR PATTERNS FOR FOUR PURSES, A JACKET, AND A CHRISTMAS STOCKING.

Boca Bag

Crazy Quilting *with attitude*

- Foundation fabric
  - Muslin 16½" x 8" (front pocket)
  - Canvas 16½" x 12" (purse back)
- Fabrics for quilting:
  - For muslin
    20" x 3" strips, 3
    10" x 3" strips, 4
  - For canvas
    20" x 3" strips, 3
    14½" x 3" strips, 2
    10" x 3" strips, 4
- Solid fabric for purse front, 15½" x 11"
- Purse bottom, 8" x 15½"
- Purse lining, 28" x 15½"
- Pocket, 13½" x 7½"
- Outer pocket lining, 7" x 15½"
- Trim for outer pocket, 15½" of brush fringe and 15½" bead fringe
- Grid to stabilize purse bottom, 6¾" square
- Handles, 36" x 4" silk, 2 pieces
- Fusible fleece for handles, 36" x ⅞", 2 pieces
- Tassel or beaded weight
- 72" x 3½" ruffled trim
- Grid pocket, 8" square
- Magnetic snaps, 2
- Silk strip 3" x 10" to cover tassel cord (optional)

This bag is a favorite OF MANY OF MY STUDENTS. IT'S A GREAT EVERYDAY PURSE.

THE PURSE BACK IS CRAZY QUILTED AND THE PURSE FRONT IS A SOLID PIECE OF FABRIC WITH A

CRAZY QUILTED POCKET TRIMMED IN BRUSH FRINGE AND BEADS. IT HAS TWO 1" HANDLES, A

MAGNETIC SNAP CLOSURE ON THE FRONT POCKET, A MAGNETIC SNAP CLOSURE INSIDE THE PURSE,

AND IS DECORATED WITH A HEAVY TASSEL OR WEIGHT. IT MEASURES 14" WIDE BY 10" TALL AND

HAS A 1¼" RUFFLE AROUND THE TOP. THE BOTTOM OF THE PURSE IS 7" SQUARE.

INSTRUCTIONS

1 To Make Handles: Fuse the fleece to each horizontal edge of each silk strip. Fold silk in half horizontally, press. Next, fold raw edges with fleece to center fold. Press. Stitch close to both sides from one end to the other. Repeat for other handle. Handle measures 1" x 36".

2 To Make Ruffle: Fold 72" x 3½" strip of fabric in half horizontally. Serge raw edges together. Manually ruffle the strip, or use a machine ruffler, Ruffle should measure 29" to 30".

3 Crazy Quilt Outer Pocket and Purse Back: Using fabric strips, quilt onto foundation fabrics diagonally, starting at center with longest strips (use crazy quilt Method 3 in Chapter 2 of this book, page 16). **Sew and flip** other pieces, using longest pieces nearest center until foundation fabric is totally covered. Trim and press. Embellish as desired (optional).

4 Trim the front piece (muslin) down to 15½" x 7". Trim the back piece (canvas) down to 15½" x 11".

5 To Make Front Pocket: First, pin beaded trim then brush fringe along one 15½" edge of smaller quilted piece. Baste close to raw edge. This is the top of pocket. Apply magnetic snap (male side only) to lining fabric as follows: Center male side of magnetic snap 1" below top edge (top edge is 15½" wide) of outer pocket lining. Use small piece of interfacing on inside of lining to secure. Pin outer pocket lining, right sides together, to same edge with beaded end of fuzzy trim. Stitch across this edge only using ½" seam allowance. Turn right side out. Press. Pocket is now finished across the top and open on sides and bottom. Machine-baste close to raw edges (or serge sides and bottom of this piece together to hold). Set aside.

Purse Assembly

1 Match bottom edge of outer pocket to bottom edge of purse front (purse front is solid fabric), lining side of pocket together with right side of purse front. Stitch along sides and bottom using ¼" seam. Apply female side of snap to purse body matching with other side of snap, which was applied to pocket lining. Use small piece of interfacing to secure. The purse front is now finished.

2 With right sides together, sew one edge (15½" side) of purse bottom fabric to bottom edge of purse front. Next, sew other edge of purse bottom fabric to bottom edge of purse back (the other quilted piece). Press seams open. At this point you should have one long piece measuring 28" x 15½". Fold this piece in half vertically, right sides together, matching top edges. Sew along side edges from top to bottom. Clip at fold close to seam. Press seam open. Miter each side at fold. To form the miter, hold the seam at the fold with one hand and match the center of the seam to the center of the purse bottom. This will form a triangle. Pin to hold this position. Mark 3½" from point. Draw a 7" line across triangle intersecting mark. Stitch across triangle on line. Set aside.

Lining Assembly

1 Make pocket by folding pocket fabric in half vertically, right sides together. Stitch around three open edges leaving small opening at bottom to turn. Turn pocket right side out and press. Stitch pocket to lining: Center pocket, fold side up, 2¾" below top edge of one end of lining piece. Stitch around three sides of pocket, leaving folded side open.

2 Apply magnetic snaps to both top edges of lining 1¼" below raw edges. (Use pieces of interfacing on inside of lining to stabilize snaps.) Fold lining in half vertically, right sides together, matching top edges.

3 Sew along one side edge from top to bottom. Sew other side edge together as follows: 5" from fold and 2" from top edge, leaving an opening to turn the purse. Clip to seam at fold so that side seams can be pressed open.

4 Miter each side at fold. See above for miter instructions. Clip triangles off leaving ½" seam allowance.

5 To make a pocket inside lining across bottom to hold grid (this step is optional): With wrong side out, press bottom square from miter on one side to miter on other side. Lay creased edge on top of 8" square of fabric cut for grid pocket. Fabric should extend about ¾" from creased edge. Stitch along fabric using hem stitch, catching lining only with hem stitch.

Putting It All Together

1 Beginning and ending at center front of purse, pin ruffle around top of purse. Baste ruffle ¼" from edge.

2 If you want to make a cover for the tassel cord (optional): Use a 3" x 10" piece of silk. Turn under 1" on one end. Fold silk strip in half lengthwise, right side together. Stitch together to form a cylinder using a ½" seam allowance. Turn right side out. Pull tassel or weight cord through cylinder. The fabric, being longer than the cord, will "scrunch" over the cord. Stitch the top of the tassel cord to the raw edge of silk.

3 Baste tassel or weight cord to center back of purse body on top of ruffle.

4 One of the two handles goes on the front of the purse, and one goes on the back of the purse. With right sides together, pin each handle end to top edge of outer purse front and back 3" from side seams. Baste ¼" from edge.

5 Before attaching lining to outer purse, make sure lining is wrong side out and outer purse is right side out. Drop outer purse into lining. Make sure handles and tassel are tucked between lining and purse. (Lining and purse should be right sides together.) Stitch around the top opening of purse. Reinforce where tassel is sewn. Clip where needed. Turn purse right side out through opening left in lining. Press around opening. Top stitch around top. Slide grid into pocket in bottom of lining. Top stitch opening in lining closed.

Yukie Bag

- Pattern (see page 127)
- Foundation fabric: canvas for quilting cut ½" larger than pattern, 2 pieces
- 14 strips of fabric (7 for purse front and 7 for purse back) for quilting in various widths as follows:
  - 7" x 13", 2 center strips
  - 3" x 13", 4
  - 2" x 13", 4
  - 2½" x 13", 4
- Lining fabric cut by pattern
- Lining bottom, 17" x 5"
- Pocket for lining, 7½" x 13"
- Purse bottom, 17" x 5"
- Front flap fabric, 6" x 9½"
- Front flap interfacing, 6" x 9½"
- Front flap lining, 6" x 9½"
- Back flap fabric, 6" x 7"
- Back flap interfacing, 6" x 7"
- Back flap lining, 6" x 7"
- Tassel trim, 2 pieces, 6" each
- Bead trim, 2 pieces, 6" each
- Magnetic snap
- Handle fabric, 4" x 36", 2 pieces
- Fusible fleece for handles, each ⅞" x 36", 4 pieces
- Plastic canvas grid, 3½" x 11"
- Grid pocket, 5½" x 10"

The Yukie Bag is an elegant purse WITH FLAPS ON BOTH THE FRONT AND BACK. THE BACK FLAP IS FOR DESIGN ONLY AND SERVES NO PURPOSE. IT HAS DOUBLE HANDLES, A MAGNETIC SNAP CLOSURE, AND IS MITERED TO CREATE A RECTANGULAR BOTTOM. IT MEASURES 10" TALL BY 10" WIDE AT THE TOP OF THE PURSE, AND 12" WIDE AT THE BOTTOM OF THE PURSE.

THE YUKIE BAG IS QUILTED A LITTLE DIFFERENTLY, USING A METHOD SIMILAR TO METHOD 3 (PAGE 16), EXCEPT THE STRIPS ARE STRAIGHT UP AND DOWN INSTEAD OF ON THE DIAGONAL.

HERE'S HOW TO MAKE THE PATTERN: CUT A PIECE OF PATTERN PAPER 11" TALL BY 17" WIDE. ACROSS THE TOP, MEASURE 1½" FROM EACH END AND MAKE A MARK. MEASURE 1½" UP FROM THE BOTTOM AND MAKE A MARK. DRAW A LINE FROM ONE MARK TO THE OTHER ON BOTH SIDES OF THE PATTERN. CUT OFF AT THE LINE.

Instructions

1 Sew strips to each piece of canvas using the sew and flip method as follows: (To help you know top from bottom, the canvas is approximately 14" wide at the top and 18" wide at the bottom. The sides are angled and are approximately 12".)

2 Place large strip vertically in center of canvas right side up. Stitch strip to canvas along both sides of strip ¼" from edges. With right sides together, place a long strip at edge and on top of strip already on canvas. Stitch using presser foot as seam guide—do not back tack. Flip and press.

3 Repeat with each strip until canvas is covered.

4 Embellish as desired (optional).

5 Press well.

6 Cut quilted pieces by pattern.

Putting Purse Together

1 With right sides together, stitch bottom edge of each quilted piece to each 17" edge of purse bottom. You will now have one long piece measuring 25" from one end to the other.

2 Fold this piece in half, right sides together, bringing raw edges together at top. On both sides, stitch from top to fold using ½" seam allowance. On both sides, clip seam allowance at fold to seam line. Do not trim seam. Press seam open.

3 Miter each side at fold. To form the miter, hold the seam at the fold with one hand and match the center of the seam to the center of the purse bottom. This will form a triangle. Pin to hold this position. Measure 2" from point. Draw a line across triangle at 2" point. This line should be 4" wide. Stitch on line. Press. Set aside.

Lining Assembly

1 With right sides together, stitch bottom edge of each lining piece to each 17" edge of lining bottom. You will now have one long piece measuring 25" x 17".

2 Apply snap. (The snap has 4 parts: There are two brass pieces each with two prongs, a male and a female, and two flat aluminum pieces with a circle in the middle and a small slit on each side of the circle.) First, make a mark at the center of both ends of lining. Fuse interfacing 1" below top edge on wrong side of lining at center on both ends. Make a 2" vertical line starting at center mark. Measure 1½" down from the top edge and make a small horizontal line across the vertical line. Use one of the aluminum pieces that comes with the snap as a template. The circle in the middle of the template should be placed at the intersection of where the lines cross. Mark both slits on the interfacing. Using a seam ripper, carefully cut slits through interfacing and fabric. Insert two prongs of one brass piece of snap through slits from the right side. Fit prongs through slits in aluminum piece. Bend prongs to secure.

3 Make pocket by folding pocket fabric in half vertically, right sides together. Stitch around three open edges, leaving small opening at bottom to turn. Turn pocket and press. Stitch pocket to lining: Center the pocket 2¼" below top edge of one end of lining piece.

4 Fold lining in half vertically, right sides together, matching top edges. Sew along one side edge from top to bottom. Sew other side edge together as follows: 4" from fold and 3" from top edge. You are leaving an opening to turn the purse. Clip near seam at fold on both sides.

5 Miter each side at fold. See step 3, Putting Purse Together, for miter instructions. Clip points off triangles, leaving ½" seam allowance.

6 To make a pocket inside lining across bottom to hold grid (optional): With wrong side out, press bottom rectangle from miter on one side to the miter on the other side. Lay creased edge on top of 5½" x 9" piece of fabric cut for grid pocket. Fabric should extend at least ¾" from creased edge. Stitch along fabric using hem stitch, catching lining with hem stitch.

To Make the Flaps (repeat for both flaps):

Sew interfacing to outer flap fabric ¼" from edge. With right sides together, sew flap lining to outer flap along one 6" edge only using a ½" seam allowance. This is the bottom of the flap. Press seam toward lining. Open these two pieces out so they are not one on top of the other. Sew trim to outer flap only from side to side just above seam. With right sides together, sew each side of lining to outer flap from seamed edge (bottom) to raw edge (top). Leave open at top. Turn right side out. Press.

To Make the Handles (repeat for both handles):

Fuse one piece of the fleece to each horizontal edge of each handle strip. Fold handle in half horizontally. Press. Next, fold raw edges with fleece to fold. Press. Stitch close to both sides from one end to the other. Handles measure 1" x 36".

Putting It All Together

1. With right sides together, baste flaps together along raw edge. Make a mark at the center of raw edge.

2. Pin "combined" flaps to outer purse. On back panel, center short flap together with right side of purse. Baste.

3. Pin the ends of one handle to one side of outer purse. Edge of handles should be 2¼" from side seam. Baste.

4. Drop outer purse into lining. Tuck handles and flaps down into lining. Lining and purse will be right sides together. Pin at seams first then ease as needed. Stitch around opening using ½" seam allowance.

5. Turn through opening left in lining.

6. Press around opening.

7. Top stitch around top.

8. Slide grid into grid pocket inside lining at bottom.

9. Top stitch opening in lining closed.

10. Press well.

Moon Pie Purse

- Pattern (on page 124)
- Foundation fabric: 2 pieces canvas cut ½" larger than pattern
- Fabric for quilting
  - 4" squares, 2
  - 3" x 10" strips, 14
- Ruffled ribbon, 28"
- 2" wide webbing for straps, 2 yds
- Beaded fringe, 31"
- Lining fabric cut by pattern, 2 pieces
- Fabric for pocket, 12" x 7½"
- Magnetic snap

This is a very easy purse to make, AND WOULD BE A FUN PROJECT FOR A NOVICE SEWER.

THE MOON PIE CONSISTS OF TWO CRAZY QUILTED PIECES SEWN WITH RIGHT SIDES TOGETHER. THERE IS NO GUSSET. BEADED FRINGE IS INSERTED IN THE SEAM JOINING THE TWO QUILTED PIECES. THE HANDLES ARE 2" WEBBING AND THERE IS A BAND OF RUFFLED RIBBON SEWN 1½" BELOW THE TOP OF THE PURSE. THE TWO LINING PIECES ARE THE SAME SIZE AS THE QUILTED PIECES.

THERE IS A POCKET SEWN ONTO THE LINING. IT HAS A MAGNETIC SNAP CLOSURE AND MEASURES APPROXIMATELY 12" WIDE BY 11" LONG.

INSTRUCTIONS

1 Crazy quilt front and back of purse on canvas. Crazy quilt by Method 1 in Chapter 2 of this book (pages 13 and 14).

2 Embellish work as desired (this step is optional).

3 Steam and press quilted pieces until very flat.

4 Cut the quilted pieces by pattern.

Lining Assembly

1 With right sides together, fold pocket in half. Stitch around three sides, leaving a small opening in the center of the bottom. Turn pocket through small opening and press.

2 Center pocket, with folded side up, on one lining piece 3½" below top edge. Stitch pocket (around pocket sides and bottom only) to lining.

3 Right sides together, stitch two lining pieces together, leaving an opening about 5" wide at bottom center. (This is where the purse will be turned after lining is sewn to quilted pieces.)

Purse Assembly

1 Insert beads between the front and back quilted panels (right sides together). Beads do not go all the way to the top of the purse. Start pinning beads 3¼" down from top raw edge, and end beads 3¼" down from the top on the other side. Stitch front and back panels of outer purse together, being careful not to sew on beads. Your seam allowance is the width of the tape to which the beads are sewn.

2 Pin the ruffled ribbon 1½" from the top edge of the purse all the way around. Overlap and turn under at end. Before sewing ribbon to purse, insert ends of each handle under ribbon. Each end of handle should be 2⅛" from side seam of purse.

3 Stitch ribbon and handles to purse.

Putting It All Together

1 With right sides together, sew lining and outer purse together around top edge using a ½" seam allowance.

2 Turn purse right side out through opening in bottom of purse lining. Press and steam around top of purse. Topstitch around top of purse.

3 Stitch opening in bottom of lining.

4 Insert magnetic snap in center under ribbon on both sides.

Church Lady Bag

- No pattern is needed for this purse, just cut pieces as follows:
- Fabric for back of purse 11" x 14"
- Strip of same fabric for band on front of purse 4" x 14"
- Fabric for purse bottom 5" x 14"
- Canvas for quilting foundation fabric, 9" x 15"
- Fabric for quilting:
  - 4" square
  - 3" x 10" strips, 12
- Plastic canvas grid to go in bottom of purse, 9" x 3¾"
- Lining, 14" x 25"
- Pocket, 7½" x 12"
- Handle, silk 6" x 36"
- Fusible fleece for handle, 1⅜" x 36", 2
- Decorative trim
- Magnetic snap

Here's a very simple bag to make WITH LOTS OF STYLE. THIS PURSE WAS DESIGNED ESPECIALLY FOR THE LADIES IN MY SUNDAY SCHOOL CLASS. WE ALL MANAGED TO FINISH THE PURSES ON A SUNDAY AFTERNOON AND THE PEOPLE WHO SING IN THE CHOIR WERE ABLE TO ATTEND CHOIR PRACTICE!

THE CHURCH LADY HAS A CRAZY QUILTED FRONT WITH A SOLID BAND AT THE TOP. THE FRONT IS DECORATED WITH TASSEL AND BEADED FRINGES. THE BACK IS A SOLID FABRIC THAT MATCHES THE BAND ON THE FRONT. I USED A LIGHTWEIGHT TAPESTRY FOR THE BAND ON THE FRONT, AND FOR THE BACK AND BOTTOM OF THE PURSE. IF LIGHTER-WEIGHT FABRIC IS DESIRED FOR THESE THREE PIECES, INTERFACING MIGHT NEED TO BE ADDED. IT MEASURES 10" TALL BY 12" WIDE.

INSTRUCTIONS

1 With 4" square and twelve fabric strips, crazy quilt on canvas using Method 2 in Chapter 2 of this book (page 15). Press well.

2 Embellish as desired. Press very well.

3 Cut quilted piece down to measure 8" x 14".

Purse Assembly

1 With right sides together, stitch 4" x 14" piece of fabric to top of quilted piece. Press seam open.

2 Apply decorative trim(s) above seam line from one side of tapestry piece to the other side.

3 With right sides together, stitch purse bottom (5" x 14") to other end of quilted piece.

4 With right sides together, stitch other side of purse bottom to fabric cut for purse back.

5 You now have a long piece measuring 14" x 25". Fold this piece in half right sides together matching top front to top back. Stitch both sides from top to bottom making sure seams match. Press seams open.

6 Make a 4" miter at bottom of purse at fold on each side seam.

7 Pin handle to both sides of outer purse centered at side seams. Baste handles to purse ¼" from edge. Set aside.

Lining Assembly

1 The lining is one piece of fabric 14" x 25".

2 Apply magnetic snaps at the center of each 14" edge of lining fabric 1½" from edges. Use a small piece of interfacing on inside of lining to stabilize snaps.

3 Fold the lining in half, right sides together, matching 14" ends. The fold is the bottom of the purse lining. Sew the folded piece together down one side from the top to the fold. Sew the other side from the top to the fold as follows: Sew down 2" from the top toward fold using a ½" seam allowance. Leave a 5" opening (this is where the purse will be turned). Finish sewing the seam from the bottom of the opening to the fold. Back tack to secure.

4 Make a 4" miter at fold at each side seam. See above for miter instructions.

Putting It All Together

1 Drop purse into lining with right sides together. Stitch around top using ½" seam allowance.

2 Turn purse right side out through opening left in lining.

3 Press around top of purse.

4 Top stitch around top of purse.

5 Top stitch closed the opening left in lining.

6 Press well.

Christmas Stocking

supplies needed

- 4" square and various strips of holiday fabric for quilting
- Canvas foundation fabric for front of stocking, cut a little larger than pattern
- Cut by pattern:
  - Lining pieces, 2
  - Velvet for back of stocking (when cutting this piece, make sure the right side is mirror image of the quilted canvas)
- Interfacing for back of stocking
- Cut by pattern for cuff:
  - Lining, 2 pieces
  - Silk for outer cuff *, 2 pieces
  - Interfacing, 2 pieces
- Silk cord for loop, 8"

*If a name is to be embroidered on the cuff, it must be done on one of these outer cuff pieces.

*½" seam allowance unless otherwise instructed.

To make this fabulous CRAZY QUILTED CHRISTMAS STOCKING, LOOK FOR A COMMERCIAL STOCKING PATTERN WITH A CUFF, OR DRAW YOUR OWN PATTERN. THE STOCKING IS CRAZY QUILTED ON THE FRONT ONLY. THE BACK IS CUT OUT OF A SOLID FABRIC, PREFERABLY VELVET. THESE DIRECTIONS CAN BE USED FOR ANY SIZE STOCKING.

INSTRUCTIONS

1 With 4" square and fabric strips, crazy quilt on canvas.

2 Embellish as desired (optional).

3 Press well and cut by pattern.

4 Cut the quilted piece down to the size of the pattern.

5 With wrong sides together, sew interfacing to wrong side of velvet back of stocking.

6 Baste cuff interfacing to wrong side of outer cuffs ¼" from edges.

7 With right sides together, sew two cuff lining pieces to the top of the outer stocking pieces (Outer stocking pieces are the crazy quilted piece and the velvet piece cut for the back of the stocking.)

8 With right sides together, sew outer cuff pieces to lining stocking lining pieces. Sew name panel (cuff) to front lining first. Make sure name cuff is right sides together with mirror image of front of stocking. The top of the name should be toward the seam joining the stocking lining to the cuff. Next, pin back cuff to back of stocking lining. Mark ⅝" from back edge of stocking lining edge. Insert loop, raw ends up.

9 With right sides together, sew front stocking lining/cuff to back stocking lining/cuff leaving opening down back of stocking lining to turn. Do not sew together across the top. Clip well around curves.

10 With right sides together, sew front quilted piece/cuff to back (velvet) stocking piece/cuff. Leave open at top. Clip well around curves. Trim around toe to ¼" from seam. Turn and press flat.

11 Pin beads around raw edges of outer cuff, right sides together. Machine baste close to the beads.

12 Drop stocking into lining. The two should be right sides together. Matching outer cuff to cuff lining, stitch cuff to cuff lining.

13 Turn stocking right side out.

14 Top stitch opening in lining.

15 Turn cuff down.

16 Press well.

17 Hand stitch any feathers or other embellishments desired around opening of stocking (optional).

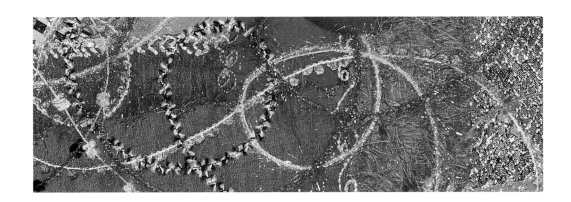

Crazy Quilted Jacket

Pick a simple jacket pattern. IT IS BEST TO CHOOSE ONE WITH VERY LITTLE DETAIL. RAGLAN SLEEVES ARE GREAT. IF YOU CHOOSE A PATTERN WITH A COLLAR, CUFFS, AND/OR PATCH POCKETS, USE A SOLID FABRIC FOR THESE PIECES. DECIDE IF THE WHOLE JACKET WILL BE CRAZY QUILTED OR IF ONLY CERTAIN PARTS WILL BE CRAZY QUILTED.

THE THING YOU NEED TO KNOW ABOUT MAKING ANY GARMENT USING THE CRAZY QUILT TECHNIQUES IS THAT YOU MUST CUT THE FOUNDATION FABRIC LARGER THAN THE PATTERN.

THE JACKET SHOWN IS MADE UP OF ONLY THREE PATTERN PIECES: THE BACK, THE FRONT, AND A RAGLAN SLEEVE. MANY PATTERNS AVAILABLE WOULD WORK WELL FOR CRAZY QUILTING ALL OVER AS I HAVE DONE ON THE JACKET SHOWN. IF YOU CHOOSE A MORE COMPLICATED PATTERN, CONSIDER QUILTING ONLY THE FRONT, OR ONLY A YOKE, OR MAYBE ONLY ONE SIDE OF THE FRONT.

ONCE THE FOUNDATION PIECES ARE CRAZY QUILTED, EMBELLISH AS DESIRED AND PRESS VERY WELL. NEXT, LAY THE PATTERN ON THE PIECES THAT HAVE BEEN QUILTED AND CUT OUT BY THE PATTERN. YOU HAVE CREATED YOUR OWN FABRIC AND NOW YOU ARE READY TO SEW THE GARMENT BY THE PATTERN INSTRUCTIONS.

IF YOU DECIDE TO LINE THE JACKET, WHICH I RECOMMEND, BE SURE TO USE VERY LIGHTWEIGHT LINING FABRIC. I LINED THE JACKET SHOWN IN THE PHOTOGRAPH WITH OLD SILK SCARVES. I JUST CUT THE SCARVES BY THE LINING PATTERN PIECES.

THIS PROCEDURE CAN BE USED TO MAKE ANY GARMENT. MANY PEOPLE MAKE VESTS. AFTER OUR SUNDAY SCHOOL CLASS MADE THE CHURCH LADY BAG, MY FRIEND DONNA LEIGH JACKINS WENT HOME AND MADE HER HUSBAND GEORGE A TIE—AND HE WORE IT!

The Sky's the Limit Gallery

After learning the art of crazy quilting, THE POSSIBILITIES ARE ENDLESS. THIS CHAPTER IS A GALLERY OF SOME OF THE WONDERFUL QUILTED PROJECTS THAT HAVE BEEN DONE AS A RESULT OF THE INSPIRATION RECEIVED FROM THE ANONYMOUS PERSON WHO CAME UP WITH THE AMAZING CRAZY QUILT CONCEPT.

THE BEST THINGS THAT HAVE HAPPENED AS A RESULT OF MY THREE-YEAR CRAZY QUILT JOURNEY ARE THE PEOPLE I'VE MET, AND THE INSPIRATION I'VE RECEIVED FROM THEM. SOME OF THE ITEMS IN MY "THE SKY'S THE LIMIT GALLERY" ARE MY OWN; HOWEVER, I AM SO PLEASED TO SHOW YOU SOME OF THE FABULOUS PROJECTS DONE BY MY WONDERFULLY TALENTED FRIENDS AND STUDENTS.

I originally designed this diaper bag for my son and daughter-in-law, Bill and Kelly Vandiver, when they were expecting their first child, Abby. This design was one of my first, and one of the most difficult. Since then, I've eased up, but the answer had to be "No" when asked if I would make more!

Celeste David, one of the "Sew & Sews," has made many of these wonderful pet beds. Our local humane society shelter has benefited from the sale of these beds because of Celeste's generosity. Art Chamblee, my friend and Sunday school teacher, made the wood frames in his woodworking shop.

Joan Brown, another of the "Sew & Sews," has been appointed "Throw Pillow Queen." Not only does Joan love making throw pillows, she's also the BEST at it!

This masterpiece was conceived and designed by Gloria Null of Meridian, Mississippi. She (along with Allison Stephens and Donna Ulmer) has made many trips to Birmingham since we all met a couple of years ago. I just have to copy her and have a crazy quilt chair in my home. She said she measured the chair and quilted the pieces larger, then took them to her upholsterer and—*voila*—instant original art that you can sit on. What a surprise we had when Gloria came in for "Square-of-the-Month," and brought this wonderful chair. We all went "crazy" over it.

Here is a smaller version of the 20" square pillow shown in Chapter 6 of this book. It measures 14" square.

Sometimes I get so enthralled with these colorful fabrics, I just want to wrap up in them. Here's a scarf for that very purpose! Model: Mrs. Jamey Freeman.

The Sky's The Limit Gallery

Virginia Lindsay, one of the "Sew & Sews," came up with this wonderful, wacky tam. Her embellishment is fabulous. Model: Morgan Freeman.

Chapter 15

Crazy Quilting *with attitude*

Interior designer and wonderful friend, Rick Stembridge, combined his painting expertise with crazy quilt abstracts to create incredible artwork for the home. He shows these paintings in his shop, Stembridge Interiors, in Birmingham, Alabama.

Here's a fun purse I designed for a trip to Boca Raton, Florida, in the summer of 2002. In the winter of 2003, we produced about 30 of these in various color combinations in classes in our B. Randle Designs Studio.

We named this creation after our wonderful "Sew & Sew," Celeste David. It's a fun purse that's easy to make.

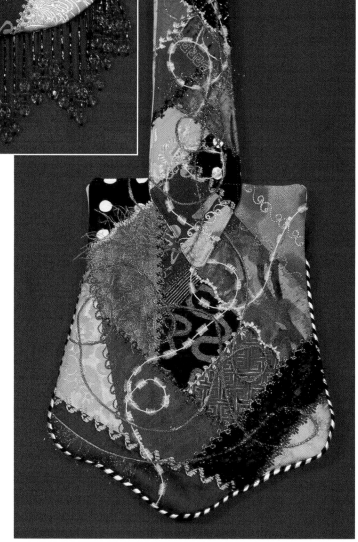

*I*n the summer of 2001, Virginia Lindsay and I went on an adventure to Washington, D.C., to the Bernina University. While there, we took a tour of the Smithsonian Presidents' Wives' exhibit. Virginia spotted two purses that were similar to these, but not crazy quilted. I stood and sketched them, and came home and made crazy quilt bags from my sketches.

Madame Butterfly

Here's a bag I put together for fun one day; it looks somewhat like butterfly wings!

Crazy Quilting *with attitude*

Virginia Lindsay used a neutral palette with exquisite embellishment … simply beautiful!

How would you like to see this wonderful bench when you go to the dentist? I'm sure Teresa Real (wife of my dentist, Pete Real) designed this bench cover just for my crazy quilt purse to rest on when I'm sitting in the examining chair at his office.

Becky Jones, a "Sew & Sew," came up with this outrageous crazy quilt window treatment, which definitely makes you smile.

Becky Jones crazy quilted these chair covers to create a beautiful corner in her house.

Becky Jones designed this great slipcover for a bench in her bedroom. She has transformed an otherwise ordinary bench into a work of art.

Patty Vann made this beautiful 36" square to go on a round side table in a guest bedroom. When I saw it, I wanted to share it in this book. What a great idea!

Becky Jones taught her daughter-in-law, April Jones, how to crazy quilt. Now, April loves to crazy quilt and is

very good at it. Becky has done just about everything you can imagine with the crazy quilt technique, but not

a table runner. April made this incredible table runner for Becky for Christmas 2002. April managed to get into

Becky's stash and get just the right fabrics to match her dining room. What a nice surprise!

TOP

LITTLE PURSE FRONT & BACK

Cut 2
Front & back (CQ)

Cut 2
lining

Fold

BOTTOM

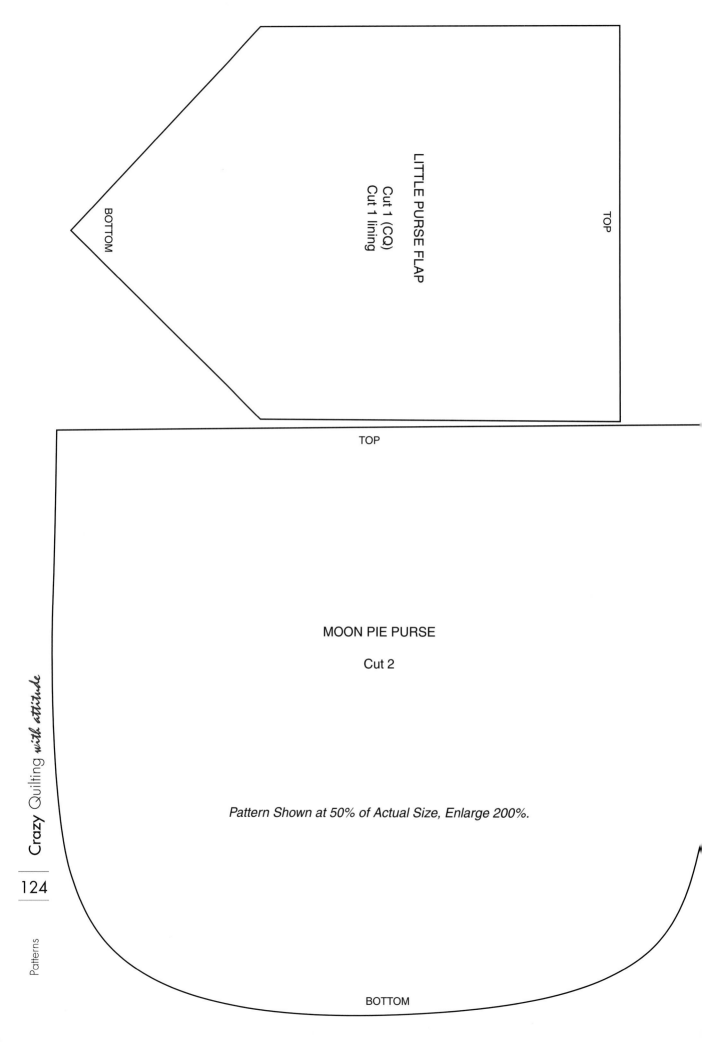

LITTLE PURSE FLAP

Cut 1 (CQ)
Cut 1 lining

TOP

BOTTOM

TOP

MOON PIE PURSE

Cut 2

Pattern Shown at 50% of Actual Size, Enlarge 200%.

BOTTOM

Crazy Quilting *with attitude*

TOP

MODIFIED MYRT HANDBAG

Cut 2
Front & back (CQ)

Cut 2
lining

Fold ▸

Cut Off Corners

BOTTOM

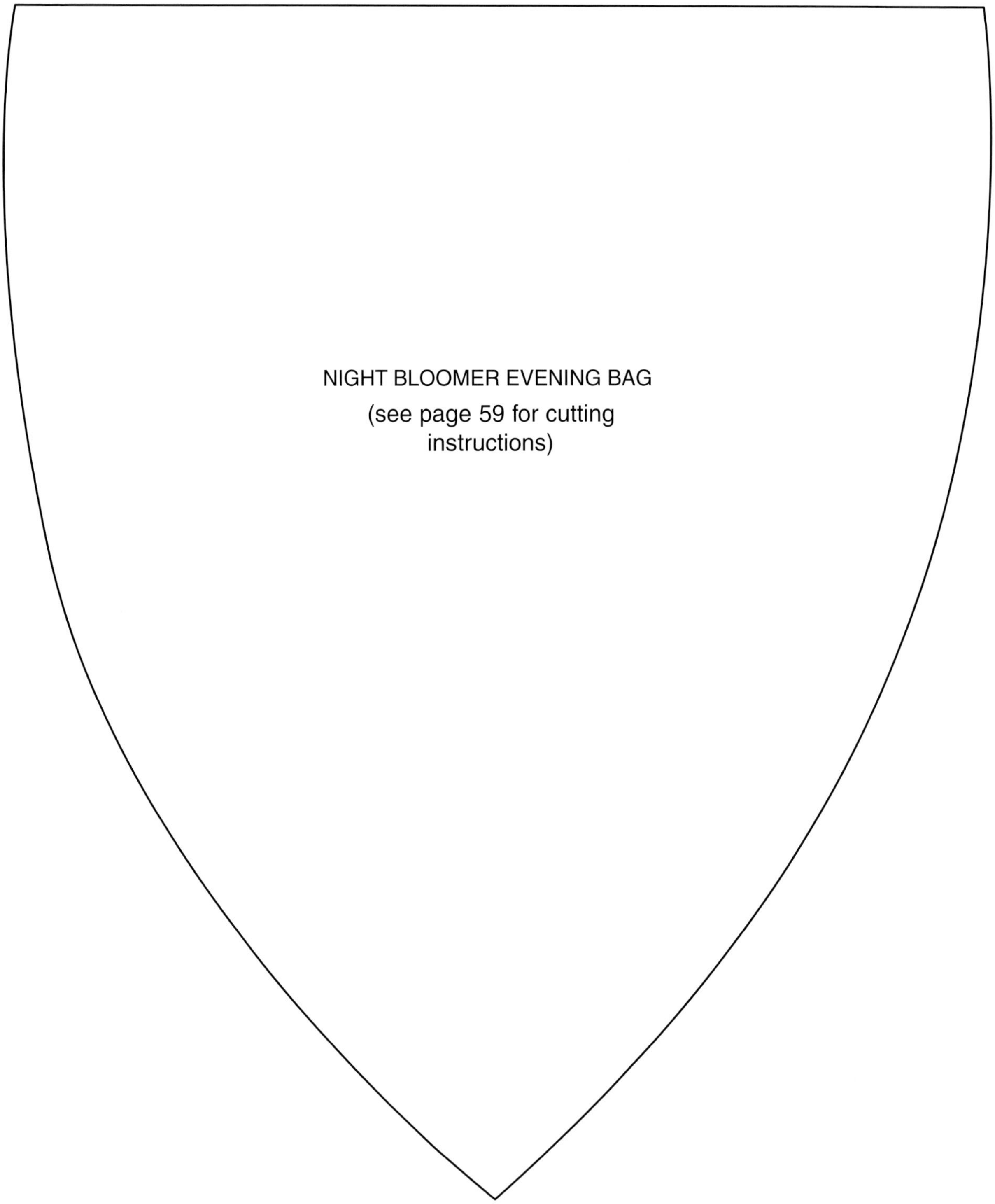

NIGHT BLOOMER EVENING BAG
(see page 59 for cutting
instructions)

Pattern Shown at 50% of Actual Size, Enlarge 200%.

PICK SAC
Cut 2
Front & back

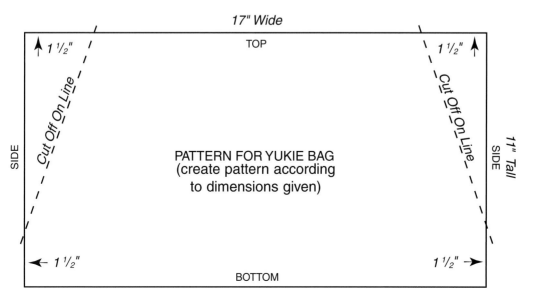

17" Wide

TOP

↑ 1 1/2"

1 1/2" ↑

Cut Off On Line

Cut Off On Line

SIDE

11" Tall
SIDE

PATTERN FOR YUKIE BAG
(create pattern according
to dimensions given)

← 1 1/2"

1 1/2" →

BOTTOM

Index